Tramline Trading

Tramline Trading

A practical guide to swing trading with tramlines, Elliott Waves and Fibonacci levels

By John Burford

HARRIMAN HOUSE LTD

3A Penns Road

Petersfield

Hampshire

GU32 2EW

GREAT BRITAIN

Tel: +44 (0)1730 233870

Email: enquiries@harriman-house.com

Website: www.harriman-house.com

First published in Great Britain in 2014 by Harriman House.

Copyright © Harriman House Ltd

The right of John Burford to be identified as Author has been asserted in accordance with the Copyright, Designs and Patents Act 1988.

ISBN: 978-0857193-95-7

British Library Cataloguing in Publication Data

A CIP catalogue record for this book can be obtained from the British Library.

Two roads diverged in a wood, and I — I took the one less travelled by,
And that has made all the difference.

Robert Frost

Free eBook

As a buyer of the print edition of *Tramline Trading* you can now download the eBook edition free of charge to read on an eBook reader, your smartphone or your computer. Simply go to:

http://ebooks.harriman-house.com/tramline

or point your smartphone at the QRC below.

You can then register and download your eBook copy of the book.

www.harriman-house.com

@harrimanhouse

www.facebook.com/harrimanhouse

www.linkedin.com/company/harriman-house

Contents

About the author

John trained as a physicist and holds a PhD in Physics from the University of Toronto. He worked for a time for NASA in Washington D.C. in the Manned Mars Exploration Team. After leaving, he discovered the financial markets and has been involved with them on and off for over thirty years. John was a Commodity Trading Advisor for a period at a Los Angeles commodities trading firm.

He has started and sold several real businesses, and now devotes full time to training, writing, trading and consulting on the markets.

John is Editor of *MoneyWeek Trader*, an email service aimed largely at UK-based spread-betters. He also operates his personal blog at **tramlinetraders.com**.

Tramline Trading Alerts Service

Many books on trading the financial markets leave you high and dry after you have finished reading. I decided to change all of that. With my Tramline Trading Alert service, you can follow what I am doing as I analyse promising trade setups.

My plan is to issue from three to five email Alerts a month, with each Alert containing several trade setups. I will cover all major currency crosses, major stock indexes, gold, interest rate futures, and an occasional individual share.

As you receive my Alerts, you will see my top trade setups come to life. This is like having me look over your shoulder as you study the markets!

Visit **tramlinetradingalerts.com** for more information and to sign up for the Alerts.

Acknowledgements

I wish to gratefully thank all of my early-year school teachers who helped shape my life, all the while suffering my in-born contrarian nature. My very first school report at the tender age of five definitively stated: "John is very erratic." I have been striving to rein in the most extreme manifestations of this trait ever since.

In the same spirit, I wish to thank all of those many traders who extracted my trading tuition fees from my early accounts. I'm sure they did not realise it, but they were performing a great service to me. Perhaps those very same traders went through an identical process themselves and considered their success also was based on their own early expensive lessons. Is there anything new under the sun?

But my most vivid trading lesson was given to me by Mark – a fellow commodity broker – who managed to short the S&P on the Friday before 19 October 1987. When the market opened on Black Monday with a huge gap down, he added to his shorts. By the close of trading, his $30k account had swelled to over half a million dollars. In 1987 that was real money! However, when the market started up on Tuesday he kept shorting on the way up. This was a fatal mistake, because the market recovered so far that he was wiped out.

So, thanks Mark, for having taught me that when I have a massive windfall profit, it is best to take at least some of those profits off the table. Also, I learned then that it is fatal to fight the market, no matter how strong your belief.

A further early lesson was provided by another former colleague, Peter, who taught me that the art of market forecasting is a vastly different skill from that of trading. Peter was an excellent predictor of trends, but constantly lost money when he traded. This was because he did not have the courage of his convictions at the right time and was always getting in too late just before a big counter-trend move.

Both Mark and Peter were futures brokers at the same commission house in Los Angeles where I cut my trading teeth. This gave me the invaluable opportunity of observing at first hand the many destructive habits that some of the firm's customers were prone to.

That was yet another lesson I learned – that trading is unlike a more conventional activity, such as being a doctor or lawyer. So my thanks to all of these customers who showed me that I had better get a proper understanding of how the markets really work, which is still today appreciated by only a fraction of people.

Finally, while writing this book I had the loyal companionship of my Jack Russell Dixie, who provided critical approval of all I wrote. All she asked in return was a daily walk at 9:30 am, prompt.

Preface

What this book covers

I am reading a book on day trading at the moment. It is full of complex indicators that may be suitable for some traders. But it is not for me. Following all of those indicators would be too confusing; I would tie myself up in knots keeping track of what all of the indicators are doing!

My method, on the other hand, allows you to have a life outside of trading. I use stop or limit orders for nearly all my trades. These can be entered in advance. And when adjustments are indicated, these can be made when you return to your screen. The market order becomes a rarity if you wish to trade in this way.

This approach has the added benefit of keeping you away from your screen where you may be tempted to change your mind (in technical jargon: to fiddle with the plan). How easy it is to watch the market move down towards your stop and exit prematurely to avoid further loss, or (an even worse sin) to widen your stop to give it a little more room. Staying away from your screen forces you to keep disciplined – an essential trait in all traders.

My tramline method should appeal to the more conservative part-time (yet serious) trader, where winning swing trades typically last for some hours to a few days at a minimum. In my case, the average holding time for a successful trade is measured in a few weeks. I have had trades that turned into monsters lasting several months. But they are quite rare and they are not my main focus; I look upon these as the icing on the cake. The bulk of my profits come from a steady accumulation of decent swings lasting a few days or weeks.

The tramline method is a simple and complete system which combines my original tramline concepts, the Fibonacci levels and basic Elliott Wave Theory. It will appeal to traders of all types, from the very beginner to the more advanced. It can apply to many markets, but I personally only trade the large currency crosses, the large stock indexes, gold and Treasury Bonds. I generally avoid individual equity markets because they can offer up sudden shocks, such as a key manager departure, or an overnight profit warning. The markets I trade do not have these disadvantages.

In the book I indicate where precise trade entry levels and stop losses can be placed. A key part of my method is to use strict money management rules which allows for low-risk trades once you have the trade setup.

Who this book is for

I have written this book for the serious trader who treats his trading as a proper business. I am assuming you know the basic mechanics of trading, the various types of orders, the markets themselves, what long and short mean, and how to read the COT (Commitments of Traders) report, which is a source of much useful information concerning the sentiment and positioning of traders.

This is not a book for the day trader. There are good methods available for such activities, but they require you to be alert to your screen throughout the trading day. This book is aimed at the time-poor trader who can (or wishes to) only devote limited time in the day to the screen.

The basis of my method is chart-reading. That is, finding recognisable patterns in charts that are reliable indicators of the next market direction. I have spent years simplifying my methods to the point where I believe that almost every willing person can quickly learn them.

I am assuming you have a basic knowledge of the principles of technical analysis (including tramlines, Elliott Waves and Fibonacci retracements).

And if you are among the group of traders who is using standard technical analysis and not achieving the results you wish for, you may be over-complicating your approach – something I studiously avoid. If this sounds like you then I suggest you go back to basics and start with my method, which uses only the simplest of elements. You can then build from there.

The structure of the book

This is a practical book which you can use to apply the principles and rules of my method. I will not devote much space to an exposition of the theories underlying my method. Since I believe a chart is worth at least a thousand words, much of the book contains charts which illustrate the various aspects of my method in real-life situations. And I include many tips and short-cuts that I have found useful in my own trading.

The vast majority of the charts are taken in real time as I wrote from November 2013 to March 2014, so I hope I cannot be accused of cherry-picking my examples. I believe this gives them a powerful immediacy. It also highlights the wealth of great trade setups that the markets are constantly offering the swing trader over just a few months. If you are following a handful of markets, you should be able to spot many possible setups in a week.

The book is divided into three parts:

In **Part I**, I develop the *tramline trading method* in the first chapter with sections on support and resistance and how to find them on any chart. And there is a section on trendlines, which is the basis of my method. Then I describe my favourite chart patterns that help me fix my trades.

In the second chapter, I explain how I use my tramline techniques to find high-probability/low-risk trades and how to manage the trades with correct stop-loss placement.

In **Part II**, I explain how you can apply my method with practical tips and ideas incorporating basic elements from Fibonacci and Elliott Wave Theory. I appreciate many traders find Elliott Wave Theory difficult to understand – identification of the waves and sub-waves can seem arbitrary. That is why I only use the very basic concepts of EW theory in my work. I believe that just a mastery of these basics will pay handsome dividends.

This part also contains practical ideas for overcoming problems we typically encounter in real-life trading. One of the most important chapters in the book is Chapter Four, where I outline my five best trading setups.

Finally, in **Part III**, I relate my day-by-day diary of two trading campaigns where I outline my analysis in real time and give the results; win, lose or draw. I hope this section will be particularly useful in showing how I set up real trades and how I manage them in the heat of the battle. I find that for most traders, trade management is the most difficult discipline to master. It is said that getting into a trade is easy, it is the getting out that is more difficult – that is where my tramline method pays dividends.

To conclude the book I offer my Eleven Commandments which, if observed, should keep you out of trouble and put you on the correct path to trading success.

Introduction

There are certain universal chart patterns that markets continue to trace out that have stood the test of time and that can be instantly recognised by a skilled trader. And when you learn how to spot these patterns and understand what they mean, then you have the basis of a solid trading method.

In this book I will show you the patterns which I have found extremely reliable that have helped me develop a complete trading system using only the most basic of elements. I call it the *tramline trading method*. It is probably one of the easiest methods to master.

I first became a student of charting in the early 1970s, well before the advent of personal computers and electronic trading. To get a market quote I needed to ring my futures broker, there was no way to keep an hourly bar chart updated in real time and I kept my paper charts updated using a pencil. Yes, it was primitive.

But what fascinated me was the fact that by examining patterns on the daily chart, I believed it possible for a reasonably skilled analyst to make a forecast of future price action. And with little or no knowledge of the fundamental supply and demand factors of the market.

The bible of charting then was Edwards and Magee* – a doorstop of a book that covered most of the classic patterns. There is a large section in the book devoted to reversal patterns and that was the part that grabbed my attention the most. In fact, because of my interest in reversal patterns, the tramline trading method I developed enables me to focus on trend changes and turning points, although not exclusively.

Early on my imagination was gripped with the possibility that if I could identify a pattern correctly, I could forecast the next likely move and I might also be able to set a price target. That was an exciting prospect. It was exciting because it would enable me to get on board a major trend early in its development before the majority had cottoned on.

But a glance at Edwards and Magee told me that charting could be a very complex area of study. The book lists a vast array of basic patterns with their many variations.

For some years I then retreated from the markets to pursue other business interests. But the siren call of the market was always there in the background. And when I felt I had achieved enough with those other businesses, I set to work on devising a simple method of analysing price charts.

The simple concept of support and resistance lines is something most students of technical analysis learn early on; I believed there could be a method that embodied this concept in a new way. I decided to base a trading method on these support and resistance lines.

---

* *Technical Analysis of Stock Trends*, by Robert D. Edwards and John Magee (CRC Press).

That is when the tramline method was born. And since working with it I have incorporated the basic ideas from Fibonacci retracements and Elliott Wave Theory to produce my complete tramline trading method.

My guiding light was to keep the method as simple as possible with no complicated maths, and to employ a minimum of tramlines on any chart. Too many lines and it gets very confusing, which is something to be avoided.

The method presented here is a complete, objective system in itself and is chart-based. *Charting* being a visual method where we look for recognisable patterns that have repeated time and time again and which help us forecast price movements with high reliability.

I believe that although my methods are simple to learn it is in the application that makes trading them challenging.

Why challenging?

It is the human factor that can make a trader override what the method is telling them. In this book I do not go into the personality hurdles that each trader faces – there are many useful volumes that already address that aspect and I do recommend you to read further on this subject. In fact, as part of my own ongoing development, I still read and study books and articles on personality and how it affects trading.

As you know, trading the financial markets is not for the dabbler or amateur. No successful trader ever takes a punt – that is for the racecourse. We are up against the smartest minds on the planet whose single-minded aim is to take our money away from us. But, with my methods, I believe you can have an edge over your opponents.

If, like me, you believe that simplicity is a means to understanding, then I hope you find some useful ideas within this book.

I have only one golden rule: keep losses small.

If you are successful in that all else follows, because your trading life will likely be a long one.

Part 1

The Tramline Trading Method

CHAPTER 1

MY CHARTING METHODS

In this chapter I will review some of the basic concepts in charting and explain how I use them with my favourite chart patterns to uncover great trade setups. The chapter has four sections:

1. Support and resistance

2. Trendlines

3. My favourite chart patterns

4. Momentum

1.1 Support and resistance

Support and resistance levels can help you identify good entry and exit points. If a market is declining into a solid support zone, the odds are good for a bounce of some sort; or if a market is rallying into overhead resistance, odds for a turn are high. And noting where the support/resistance levels are located can give you added confidence in a trade that you have identified by other methods.

Because support and resistance zones are derived from previous price action, it is clear that markets have **memories.** Markets remember the price levels where traders have previously established their positions and current price patterns are influenced by them. I will explain how this works in this chapter.

I use four different types of support/resistance levels:

1. horizontal support/resistance levels in congestion zones

2. trendlines (sloping lines of support/resistance)

3. Fibonacci retraces

4. chart support/resistance

We will now look at these in detail.

1. Horizontal support/resistance levels

The horizontal support/resistance zone is one of the most basic of charting patterns. One major feature of these levels is that a support line transforms into a line of resistance after the market has penetrated the support (and *vice versa*). Figure 1.1.1 is a great example of support/resistance areas in gold.

FIGURE 1.1.1

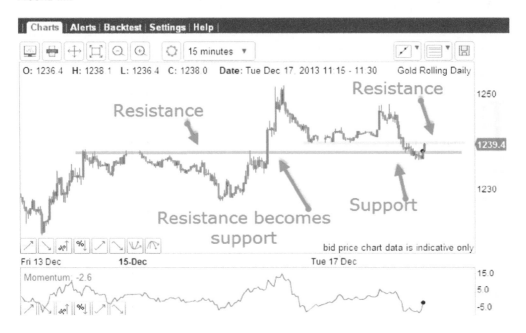

This is the 15-min gold chart and the resistance level of $1238 is clearly visible with several high touch points between 14 and 16 December. Then, the attempt to break up through the resistance on 16 December was successful with many buy-stop orders being triggered. Many chartists note these resistance levels and place their protective buy stops just above this level. These are the buy-stops of the shorts that are hit when the resistance is overcome. There are also entry buy-stops placed there by those traders looking to be long on such an upward break. After those buy orders were filled the market fell back in a normal re-test and the resistance zone then became a support zone.

On 17 December, the market fell back to test the new support zone. This held and the market proceeded to test the resistance zone. This zone was created by the lows at the $1240 level.

When those lows were broken, sell stop-losses were touched. So now, the market is trading between a narrow support and a resistance zone and will break out of it in due course.

So what were the internal dynamics of the market in this period and why does a resistance line turn into a line of support?

I will start with the idea that the current market price is determined by only a small number of traders. It takes only one buyer and one seller to make a price. When you have taken a position either long or short, you have no more influence on the price until you decide to trade again.

So, because short-term players will be trading much more frequently than position traders, these short-term traders determine the short-term price patterns. Many will be trading several times a day. Because these traders are shooting for relatively modest gains per trade, they also limit losses on losing trades.

Let's take a trader who noted the initial resistance at $1238 and decided to short the market when it reached that level again. With the breaking of this resistance on 16 December, that trade is a loser. When the trader sees the market get away from him as it rallies to $1250, he knows he has a losing trade and will naturally seek to exit his trade if the market gets back to near his entry, thus enabling a smaller loss.

In addition, there will be traders who look to go long on a decline to the $1240 support and this will compound the buying pressure.

That is why, when the market retreated to the $1240 level, many shorts are covered and new longs initiated, thereby providing buying support. Similarly, when the market broke the $1240 support, it got back to the $1238 area and more buying emerged by the shorts who had a losing trade previously. Figure 1.1.2 shows how that played out.

FIGURE 1.1.2

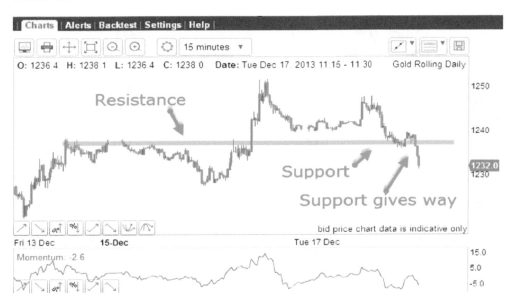

The resistance at the \$1240 level was strong enough to turn the budding rally back on 17 December. And then the \$1238 support level was breached. The market then fell under sustained selling by the disappointed bulls. The bears had won.

A short trade could be made on the break of the support low in the \$1236 area because with the break, the previous support line now becomes resistance. Any rallies should be contained by this resistance in the \$1238 area. This enables a protective stop to be entered just above this level for a low-risk trade.

I have just described a short-term support and resistance setup with horizontal zones. We can also find horizontal support and resistance zones in longer-term charts.

Figure 1.1.3 shows the weekly FTSE 100. The top bar in this chart is a seven-year resistance zone, and the bottom zone is both resistance and support (at various times). The most recent decline in June 2013 was contained by the seven-year support zone, and the most recent highs are being contained by the seven-year resistance zone.

I hope you find this an impressive demonstration that markets have long memories. It is a theme I will keep coming back to. The 6,000 and 6,800 areas are very important for the FTSE 100, which means that if the market gets back to either of these levels, it will be well worth noting for a possible long-term trade setup.

FIGURE 1.1.3

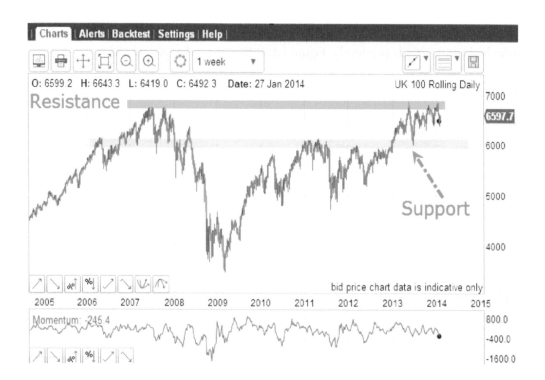

2. Trendlines (sloping support/resistance)

The trendline is another very basic element of charting. It is the basis of my tramline method, which I cover in detail in Section 2.1.

If we consider a bull market, the price pattern is a series of moves up and down but travelling generally in an upwards direction with higher highs and higher lows.

It is a curious fact that often the lows of these waves can be connected by drawing a straight line between them. Why this phenomenon exists is a mystery and most of us take it for granted.

An example is shown in Figure 1.1.4.

FIGURE 1.1.4

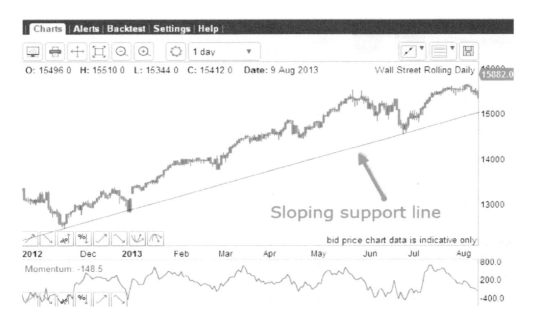

There were the two major lows in 2012 and I have drawn a straight line between them and extended it. This is a line of support in a bull market. Months later in June the market made a major low **right on the line** and then resumed its uptrend. The market had remembered the previous lows and bounced off this line of major support, which was set on the chart months previously.

But not all trendlines have such accurate touch points.

How do I find the best fit for a trendline?

To help answer this, I will briefly explain why I prefer candlestick charts to bar charts.

The reason for this relates to candlesticks containing what I call *pigtails* – the thin lines above and beneath the solid body of the candlestick.

Figure 1.1.5 will help me to describe what I mean.

FIGURE 1.1.5

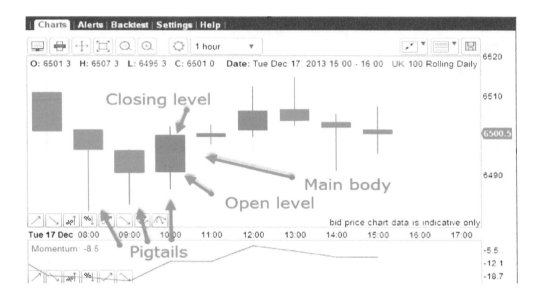

On the 10:00 am candlestick, the bottom of the body is the opening price for that hour and the top of the body is the closing price for that hour. The low of the pigtail is the lowest price in that hour. This pigtail may have been a spiky move – a quick down and then up as stops are hit and the dip is supported. For me, the most important section of trading is between the opening and closing prices – in other words, the thick body of the candle. And this section is most readily visible on a candlestick.

For this reason, I sometimes (but not always) crop off the pigtails when I look for trendlines.

A great example is shown in Figure 1.1.6. Here, I crop the upper pigtail where marked because my line makes a better fit on the lower touch point and I now have three touch points (the more touch points the better). My job in trendline placement is to make the best fit for the available highs or lows.

Does it matter how precisely you draw the trendline?

The answer is: it all depends. If you are looking for a reversal from a down-sloping trendline, you would be placing your entry buy stop just above the trendline, hoping to catch a sharp rally taking the market through your stop. In the above example, being too accurate was not necessary because the rally was sharp.

However, if you are looking to trade with the trend and enter the market at or very close to the trendline, being accurate in trendline placement is necessary when seeking a low-risk trade. I shall show some examples in the next section.

FIGURE 1.1.6

Now, back to looking for trendlines.

When starting to look for a trendline I always start with the top (or bottom) tick and swivel my line until I can visually line up at least one other accurate touch point. If I have more than one accurate touch point, then I can usually say that I have my best fit.

But, if not, then I must compromise even if it means cutting off pigtails.

In the example shown in Figure 1.1.7 I have two alternative trendlines. The line starting at the extreme high on 30 November cuts off pigtails on 10 December but includes the latest high as an accurate touch point. That is good.

The other line cuts off the pigtail on the 30 November high and includes the accurate touch point on 10 December, but misses by a wide margin the latest highs. If you were trying to line up a short trade near this line, you may have missed an opportunity.

FIGURE 1.1.7

Sadly, there is no easy answer to the question of trendline placement when the absolute highs (or lows) do not exactly line up. But when we examine the equivalent **tramline placement**, it often clears up this question. Which trendline ought to be drawn on the chart in Figure 1.1.7 is cleared up using tramline placement in Section 2.2.

Figure 1.1.8 provides a great example in gold (which is a market notorious for pigtails).

There are several options for the upper tramline placement in Figure 1.1.8. So I start with the lower tramline instead. And here, I have an accurate tramline complete with a pigtail cut-off. There really is no other way to place this tramline. It has two accurate touch points and a pigtail cut-off.

With this tramline now fixed, I can then draw in the upper parallel tramline as shown. Previously, the upper tramline had options, but with the lower tramline in place, the upper line is now set. It starts from the absolute high at the top, left-hand arrow (in fact, it is a double touch point) and there are two other widely-spaced accurate touch points.

The second upper arrow points to an overshoot. Overshoots do not necessarily invalidate a trendline, but if there are more than two big ones, I would not use that trendline. The line has four touch points, making this tramline a secure line of resistance.

It is quite rare – and reassuring when it does happen – to find more than three or four touch points lining up accurately on a trendline. You must allow some leeway.

12

FIGURE 1.1.8

Using a pair of parallel tramlines in this way enables me to place both lines accurately. I will discuss this in more detail in Section 2.2.

Trendline fitting

The rule I adhere to is this: the more accurate the fit, the more confidence I can have in the tramline (or tramlines) as a reliable line of support/resistance.

---

3. Fibonacci levels as potential support/resistance

The Fibonacci tool on your charting package is one of the most important in your toolbox. I use the Fibonacci levels to anticipate market turns. They can be remarkably accurate, enabling you to enter tight protective stops for a low-risk trade, provided this is indicated from additional analysis.

The only decision you have to make is from which pivot points to draw the Fibonacci levels. By pivot point, I mean the high and the low that are chosen to divide into the various Fibonacci levels.

How can I find the best pivot points?

I have found that the pivot points that usually work best are the most recent significant high and low. But these may not always get the best results. You see, we are looking for the best fit of the lines to the highs and lows **between** the pivot points. Sometimes this is obtained when the second significant high/low is used.

To start the search for the best fit, I always go for the most recent high and low as my pivot points to test my Fibonacci levels. Figure 1.1.9 helps to show what I mean.

FIGURE 1.1.9

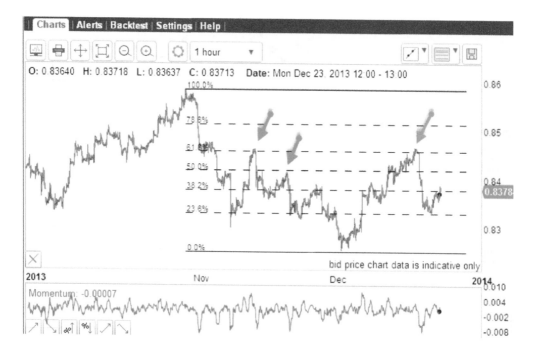

Here, I have used the major high and low as pivot points and right away I see that the two major intervening highs are made at the Fibonacci 62% and 50% levels (indicated with the first two arrows as you read from the left). This occurs before the low pivot point is put in. Then, on the rally, the market was turned at the Fibonacci 62% level (most right-hand arrow). The fact that the market made those accurate hits (left-hand arrows) previously increased my confidence that the subsequent rally would likely turn at a Fibonacci level.

Does using the extreme high/low always give the best fit?

Sometimes, using the extreme high or low for pivot points does not give you the best fit. By this I mean none of the intermediate highs/lows lying between the pivot points do not lie easily on the various Fibonacci levels. To make a best fit, I need to see at least one major high/low accurately touch a Fibonacci level. An example is shown in Figure 1.1.10.

FIGURE 1.1.10

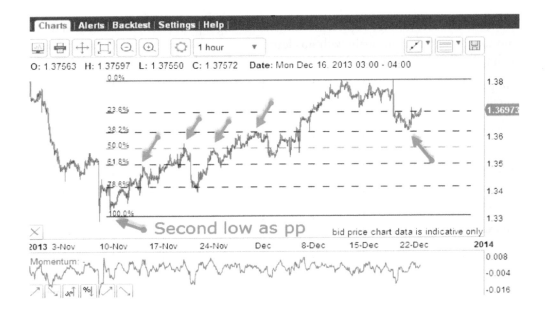

Here, I have used the second major low as pivot point (pp) and note the accurate hits on the Fibonacci 62%, 50% and 38% levels on the way up to the high pivot point (these hits are marked with the first four arrows as you read from the left). And to confirm this choice, following the high the market declined to an exact hit on the Fibonacci 38% support level (marked by the most right-hand arrow). That was a low-risk trade entry level.

Note that I had four earlier arrows and four accurate hits. Having four hits gives me great confidence I have selected the correct pivot points.

My rule of checking the second pivot point as well as the major high/low only applies to the earliest pivot point, not the latest one. In fact, this second high/low is often a wave 2 (w2) in a five-wave sequence (see Section 3.8 for Elliott Wave analysis). As it happens, in the above example the rally is not a clear five-wave impulse pattern.

I will always check these alternative pivot points in this way for my best fit. In general, the more accurate the hits are by the intermediate highs/lows, the more confidence I will have that I have my best fit. Of course, if the market has made an accurate hit on a shallow Fibonacci level after the most recent pivot point has been made, and the market then digs deeper into the retracement, the approaching Fibonacci levels will give me high confidence that turns will be made at one of them.

4. Chart support/resistance

In traditional charting, a *congestion zone* is an extended period of trading which takes place in a relatively narrow range of prices. The market swings up into resistance and then down into support and then up again with no clear direction. This can drive you mad if you are trading breakouts and you can be whipsawed to death on the false breakouts.

Congestions zones are very common in charts in all time scales. They represent a kind of equilibrium between the bulls and the bears with neither having an upper hand in that period.

What typically occurs when the market breaks out of a congestion zone?

When the market does manage to break away from a congestion zone and approaches it again, the market is often turned away from the edge of the zone. In other words, the outer limits of the congestion zone act as support/resistance, whereas before it was resistance/support.

An example is shown in Figure 1.1.11.

FIGURE 1.1.11

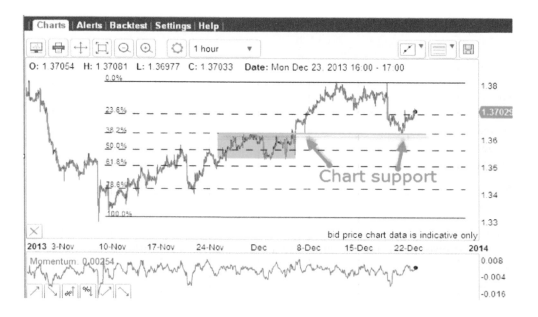

The congestion zone is highlighted. Within the zone, every time the market approached the lower and higher limit, it was turned back. These limits acted as support and resistance. Then the market broke up out of the zone. When it tried to fall back into it, it hit support at the upper limit. The market then climbed away, but when it declined off the 1.38 level, it hit support again at the upper congestion zone level.

This support level was previously resistance when the market was trading inside the zone. I call this *chart support* and it is another result of the market having a memory.

Figure 1.1.12 shows another example where there is a small false breakout of the congestion zone, which has broken to the downside. Now, the market is trying to rally back and has hit the underside of the zone. This level is now resistance where previously it was support.

FIGURE 1.1.12

With no other knowledge, a short trade here might seem a good trade as the market had rallied into resistance and the next move should be down.

So, was this an advisable trade?

To answer that question we must always consider the *context* of the trade in question (see Section 3.9). Analysing the Elliott Waves (EW) from the top, my wave labels are shown in Figure 1.1.13.

Before the break of chart support, I can count waves 1, 2, 3, and 4. Wave 3 is strong to the downside (the strongest (lowest) momentum reading occurs within this wave, which is a guideline of Elliott Wave Theory) and there is a budding positive momentum divergence at my wave 5 low, confirming that a turn up is very likely.

FIGURE 1.1.13

With this knowledge, you should be expecting at least some upward retracement of the decline off the w5 low; thus the suggested short trade was not advisable because *fifth waves are ending waves*. Of course, before the w5 low was made, I had no evidence there would be a momentum divergence, but since I could count four waves and infer the fifth lay just ahead, I could give this trade a pass.

Another great example of what I mean by understanding context is shown in the Tesco chart in Figure 1.1.14.

Tesco has rallied and has entered a definite congestion zone of trading with the price confined between the two support and resistance bars on this daily chart. And now it has broken up out of congestion.

Is this a good long trade signal?

Once again, I always look for context at any possible Elliott Wave count within the current wave. My normal routine is to start at the low and work upwards in a bull trend (opposite for a bear trend). I can count perhaps waves 1 and 2 and the long and strong wave has all the hallmarks of a third wave (see Figure 1.1.15). In fact, whenever I see a long and strong move, I always suspect I have a third wave. That is my starting point on many charts.

FIGURE 1.1.14

If I have the first three waves labelled correctly and the last touch on the support line is my wave 4, then the breakout could well be a fifth (and ending) wave. I do not want to be trading long into a fifth and final wave up! And sure enough, my suspicions were confirmed that the wave 5 breakout was a false buy signal, as you can see in Figure 1.1.15.

So, I have a complete five waves up and the next move is down. This Elliott Wave interpretation was aided by the large negative momentum divergence on the breakout. In fact, the wave 5 breakout was a sell signal, since fifth waves are best traded by fading them.

If I had gone long on the upside breakout in wave 5, I would be nursing a heavy loss on the gap down.

This is an excellent example of how, by reading the relevant Elliott Waves, you can avoid common pitfalls.

FIGURE 1.1.15

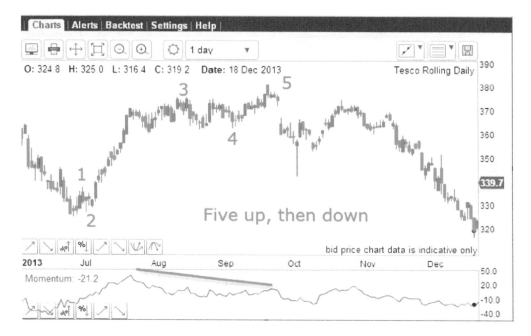

Another great example of reading Elliott Waves to inform your trading decisions can be seen in the very long-term chart of AUD/JPY in Figure 1.1.16.

FIGURE 1.1.16

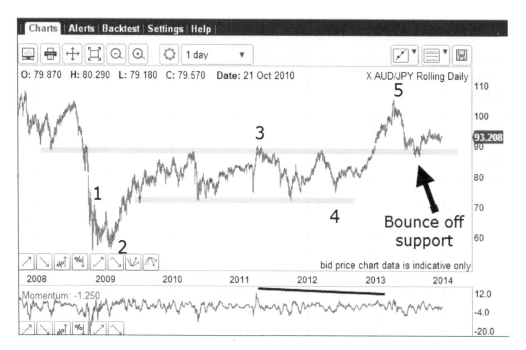

From the 2008 low, the market rallied and entered a multi-year congestion zone which has very precise support and resistance levels. The congestion zone is a wide one of over 1000 pips and offered multiple opportunities for swing traders. The zone was formed from the resistance level provided by the low in early 2008 and the support just above the 70 area.

But in early 2013, the market managed to make a break up from the zone.

We must always ask the question: is this a genuine break or a false move?

A genuine break would involve a major new bull run – preferably in a third wave – to above the highs of 2007/8. A false breakout would infer a decline back to support and perhaps the start of a new bear run.

At this upward break, the Elliott Wave labels are clear and the breakout is a fifth wave into 2013. That is not to say a long trade was inadvisable. On this scale, the rally carried by over 1000 pips in a few months – a very substantial move for a swing trade.

Then the market topped out in the 105 area and dropped back towards the congestion zone, but found good support when it hit the extension of the previous resistance level from the congestion zone. This is a textbook example of a long-term resistance level transforming into support after its upward penetration. That was a good area to look for a new long trade. The downside risk was low because of the strong support.

Finally, Figure 1.1.17 is a chart showing the congestion zone as a **continuation pattern**.

FIGURE 1.1.17

Here is the context: I am unable to place Elliott Wave labels on the decline and to me, it is clear this zone is not a wave 3/wave 4 combination as in the above examples. This allows the possibility to take a short trade on a break of support with confidence, since the trade would be trading with the trend (down).

Summary

1. I look for **four types of support/resistance**:

    i.   Horizontal

    ii. Sloping (trendlines and tramlines)

    iii. Fibonacci levels

    iv. Chart support/resistance in congestion zones

2. **Markets have memories** – that is why the notion of support and resistance occurs. Be watchful when the market is entering an old area of support/resistance.

3. Always judge the **context of the pattern** within waves, especially if the Elliott Waves can be readily discerned.

4. Watch for **false breakouts**, especially if in the fifth wave position. You can look to fade these. This applies especially when dealing with chart congestion zones.

5. In general, when the market is **descending into a support zone**, look to trade long. And when it is **ascending into a resistance zone**, look to trade short. But try to find other reasons for the trade from tramlines or Elliott Wave analysis.

6. Always **apply the Fibonacci levels** when you have a major high and low in place. These will give you the most likely turning points for any counter-trend move, and the 50% and 62% levels are the most common. Try for a best fit with the second major high/low as the earliest pivot point. This may make the intervening highs/lows lie more accurately on the various Fibonacci levels. When several minor intervening highs/lows lie on the Fibonacci levels, you can have high confidence in them as future support/resistance levels.

1.2 Trendlines

Trendlines are the backbone of my method. They are the straight lines joining either the lows or the highs in a chosen period of trading with no market moves either *above* the line (in the case of joining the highs), or *below* the line (in the case of joining the lows). The highs and lows in a chart define the various waves which may be suitable for swing trading.

Because markets have memories, trendlines appear very often on charts of all time frames. However, in my experience it is rare for all of the highs/lows in any chart to line up perfectly accurately and the greater the number of highs/lows the more often we must resort to tweaking the line for a best fit.

Figure 1.2.1 shows an example in EUR/USD.

FIGURE 1.2.1

Here is a textbook trendline. I have three highly accurate touch points that are reasonably evenly spaced and a couple of near-misses along the way. This makes it a highly reliable line of support/resistance. Note that in the period to the late December break, this line acted as solid support with no trading taking place under the line.

And when the trendline was broken to the downside, the move was quite sharp as the line then became a line of resistance, forcing prices lower.

When you have a very reliable trendline such as this, and when the market does eventually break through it, this is usually a genuine break giving you a high-confidence trade. The trade could have been placed with a resting short sell order placed just under the trendline.

Now here is a not-so-good trendline, shown in Figure 1.2.2.

I have only two touch points (the arrows) and a pigtail touch (the bar). There are not enough accurate touch points to call this a highly reliable trendline. And the performance beyond the break is all over the map! The market swerves up and then down around the line, confirming the line as unreliable as a line of support/resistance following the break.

FIGURE 1.2.2

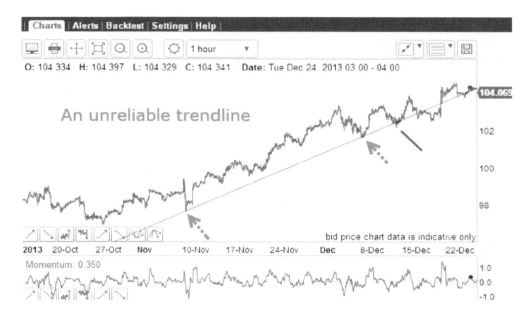

How many accurate touch points do I need for a reliable trendline?

I like to see at least three accurate touch points (or nearly so) to confirm I have a solid trendline that I can use as a basis for trading. Sometimes, this involves chopping off a pigtail to get the best fit (as we began to look at earlier).

Figure 1.2.3 shows a good example in GBP/USD.

Using the lows, I have five accurate touch points (with one small pigtail), thus making this a reliable line of support/resistance. This was confirmed when the market rallied back to the line after the break to plant not one but two kisses on the underside of the line before peeling away.

FIGURE 1.2.3

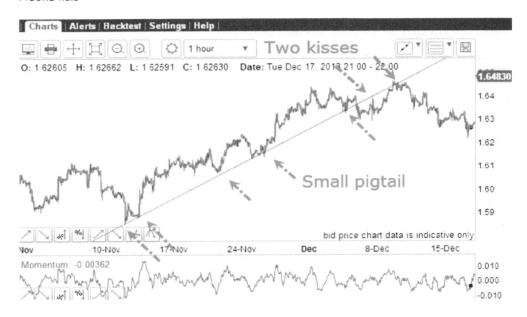

But was that the only trendline joining the lows I could have drawn on this chart?

Let's explore this, using Figure 1.2.4.

FIGURE 1.2.4

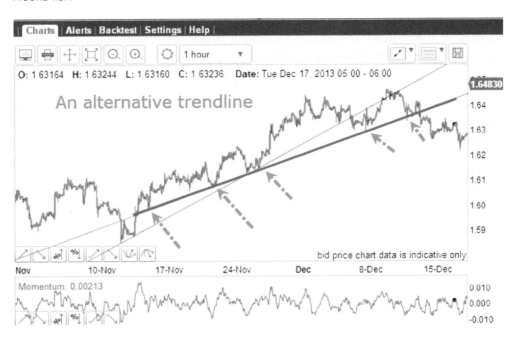

I do have another trendline candidate for this chart (shown using the thicker, purple line), and it also has five accurate touch points. This makes it a reliable trendline. But in this one, there is no kiss after the trendline has been broken.

We can therefore use either one of these trendlines with confidence and a break of either would give us a short sell signal.

But which will be our primary line will be discovered when we search for its partner in the tramline pair. We shall look at this in Section 2.2.

The point I want to make is this: it is quite common to find alternative trendlines of equal merit on the same chart. And each one can be used for trading.

1.3 My favourite chart patterns

There are four classic chart patterns that I search for and trust. They are all quite easy to spot when they are in progress in their completion phase. These patterns are:

1. Head & Shoulders
2. Triangles and Wedges
3. The Five-Wave Continuation
4. The Key Reversal

1. Head & Shoulders (H&S)

This is a classic **reversal pattern** that is sometimes seen at the end of a long trend, though not all trends terminate in an H&S. Many technicians erroneously assign this pattern in the middle of a swing move, or not at the end of a major run. In my experience, the true Head & Shoulders occurs infrequently. I look for it especially on the daily and hourly charts and it can be seen in both after a long rally or a long decline.

A good example is shown in Figure 1.3.1 on the hourly chart of the T-Bonds.

After a solid down-trending phase, the market made a low in the **Left Shoulder** (LS), then rallied but couldn't hold it and dropped to a new low to the **Head**, rallied again but couldn't hold that and then declined – **but not to a new low** – in the **Right Shoulder** (RS). From there, it rallied and broke through the **Neckline** (the line joining the minor highs between the Head and the two Shoulders).

FIGURE 1.3.1

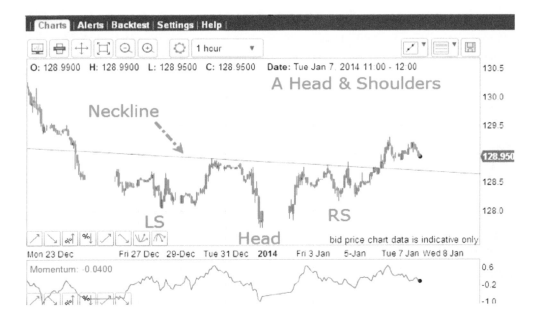

How do I trade the H&S?

The Neckline break has confirmed the **reversal pattern** and now the market will likely come back down to test the Neckline in a kiss. There are two candidates for a long trade entry: at the Neckline break and at the testing of the Neckline at the kiss. Placing a buy-stop entry just above the Neckline is my preferred trade entry method. Provided the market breaks above the Neckline, that guarantees a position. The market often moves very sharply from these patterns and you will have a good entry using this method.

The other technique is to wait for the market to test the Neckline after the break has occurred. What I am looking for is a kiss on the line and a Scalded Cat Bounce (see Section 3.6) up and away. The problem here is this: the kiss may not happen! The market could simply take off on the upside without you. But if you miss it, you miss it – move on. You may get another low-risk opportunity later. At least you have identified an H&S reversal and the trend should now be firmly established and you can use your usual methods from there.

If we took the long trade on the Neckline break, we could place our protective stop just below the RS. This is a very sensible place, since a break of this level would very likely cancel out the H&S pattern and the market would likely continue lower, where we would not want to be long.

How did this trade develop?

Figure 1.3.2 shows the chart a few days later, where we can see the move up and away from the H&S pattern.

FIGURE 1.3.2

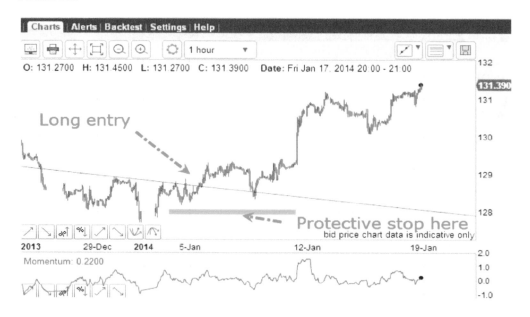

The market did retreat to test the Neckline in a kiss (with a slight overshoot), but staged a vigorous rally in a Scalded Cat Bounce. That was a nice confirmation of the H&S bottom.

Figure 1.3.3 provides another example in the hourly chart of the Hong Kong Stock Index.

FIGURE 1.3.3

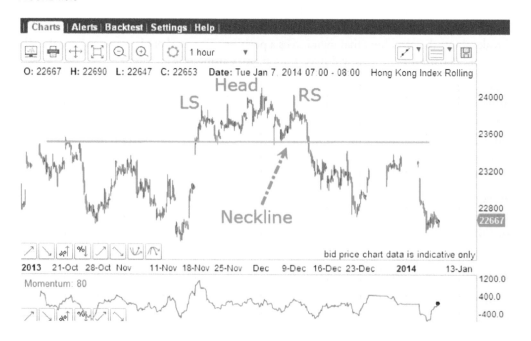

The market had been in a strong rally phase and in mid-November had made a new high for the move. It then traced out a lovely complex Head & Shoulders with the horizontal neckline also lying on chart support from the previous minor high of 21 October. But in early December, the market made a bold break of the Neckline, thus confirming the H&S pattern. The Neckline then became a line of resistance. Note that the rallies back to the line failed to kiss it, which indicated an underlying weakness.

Why is a kiss failure important?

Whenever the market suffers a kiss failure to a reliable line of resistance/support, that is a sign the market likely wants to move sharply away. I use this observation as a major signal of market weakness. Kiss failures are well worth noting. I cover this point in Section 3.6.

In this case, waiting for that kiss to give you an entry would have proved futile and the best entry method was to place a resting sell-stop just under the Neckline. Most of the time, this will be the favoured entry method. Its great benefit is that you do not need to be watching the market and waiting for the break. When the H&S pattern is well developed, you can anticipate the Neckline break and place your orders ahead of time.

Can I trade this setup using resting stop orders?

When trading neckline breaks, you can place your resting stop order quite close to the neckline. If it is a genuine neckline break, the market should move away in your direction promptly. This means you can place your protective stop just on the other side of the neckline in case the market reverses. This would give you your low-risk trade. But check the pip differential first to ensure it is within your risk tolerance.

One point to bear in mind with resting orders: keep track of them because if they go unfilled, they are forever lurking on your trading platform and may be unexpectedly activated at an inconvenient time much later. My practice is this: if they are not touched in the time frame for the trade I have in mind, then I cancel the order.

And how did this trade develop?

Figure 1.3.4 shows the daily chart, where we can see a new larger H&S pattern working.

The H&S pattern in the hourly chart is now the head of a larger H&S pattern, which was confirmed on the neckline break. Isn't that pretty? Two H&S patterns for the price of one!

Trading the first H&S and a short in the 23,500 area would now be in considerable profit with last quote at 21,480 for a gain of over 2,000 pips.

FIGURE 1.3.4

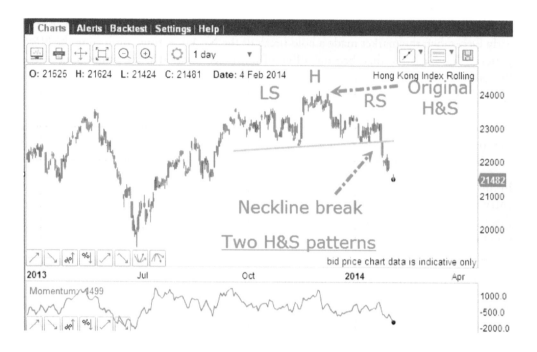

Price target rule

In an H&S, the **minimum** price target is given by the equality of the vertical price distance of the Head from the neckline and the target from the Neckline.

In our current example, this gives a target of 21,480 and as we can see in Figure 1.3.5 the market made a direct hit on the H&S target before staging a bounce. This confirms the idea of taking a profit at the 21,480 level.

FIGURE 1.3.5

This following example in the France CAC Index (Figure 1.3.6) illustrates why searching for H&S reversal patterns can reap big rewards. Again, it allows you to project a **minimum** price target well in advance.

After a long decline, the market made its low in the Head with a positive momentum divergence, suggesting the downtrend was about to end. The Right Shoulder which, although it is much smaller in size than the complex Left Shoulder, is roughly of the same scale and is usable. When the Neckline was broken, that confirmed the H&S pattern.

I can now draw some tramlines on the chart (I will properly explain the drawing of tramlines in Sections 2.1 and 2.2). Given the Head is the sole touch point for the lowest tramline, I draw an equidistant upper tramline – and that gives me the **minimum** price target for the rally. The market did in fact rally to that line and then backed off after hitting the target. The market respected that price level as resistance.

So not only did I have a minimum target from my tramline measure, but also from the H&S measure. That doubled my confidence in this target. Whenever I identify a reliable H&S pattern, I always evaluate the minimum target, which becomes my first target.

The difficulty in detecting this pattern is deciding where the neckline should be placed in real time. Looking at the above chart and the rally up off the Head, it is unclear if this is to become a true H&S pattern; there simply is not enough information yet. Then, as the rally builds, the market makes a succession of minor highs and lows. Which minor high should be used for the Neckline touch point?

FIGURE 1.3.6

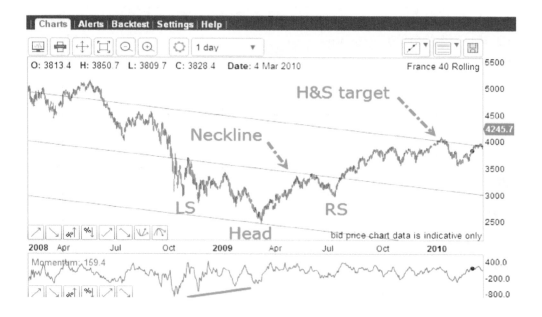

How can I find the true neckline in real time?

At this juncture, you just have to keep adjusting your Neckline until you see a dip that is large enough to be called a Shoulder. Minor dips usually do not qualify. The scale of the two shoulders should be roughly equal. But here, the dip in early July is the largest since the Head was put in (and had an A-B-C Elliott Wave form) and thus qualifies as a potential RS. Just go ahead and apply the Neckline across the minor highs as shown. Then, when the Neckline is broken, that is your signal that you have a high-probability candidate for a H&S, thus giving you your trade entry point and first target.

One further point: finding a Head & Shoulders pattern on the weekly and daily charts is good, and even on the hourly chart, but I would not trust the H&S on any chart of time scale less than hourly.

I like to see a momentum divergence (see Section 1.4) between the Head and LS. There is one in the Hong Kong Index and the France CAC examples above.

2. Triangles and Wedges

These patterns are common in all time frames and usually precede sharp moves.

Trading triangles

The triangle is a pattern where the lines joining the highs and the lows converge. Also, the upper line must slope down and the lower line must slope up or be horizontal. Triangles and wedges are in reality zones of congestion. You will find many tradable triangles in a typical week. Figure 1.3.7 shows an example in IBM.

FIGURE 1.3.7

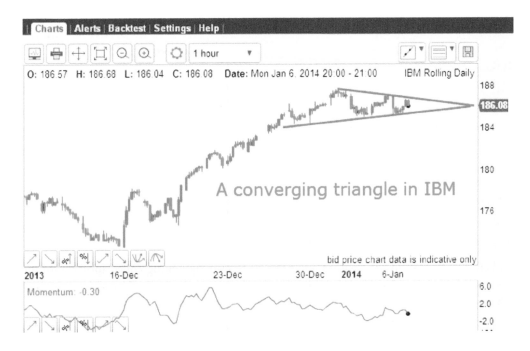

The market has made a strong rally, but now indecision has crept in after such strong gains. The market is not making new highs and the lows are being contained by the lower line of support. At some point, the market will break out of this period of consolidation/congestion and may be traded accordingly.

This is a fine example of a triangle – which could morph into a Head & Shoulders if the market breaks below the lower triangle support line. That would give additional support to a change of trend forecast. But don't jump the gun. It is better to let the market speak, which it will when one of the lines is broken.

A large triangle in the Nikkei is shown in Figure 1.3.8.

FIGURE 1.3.8

A large triangle in Nikkei

This triangle was formed over a month during which the pressure had been building for an explosive move. When the market broke the upper resistance triangle line, it took off.

Look on a triangle as a tightly-coiled spring ready to unwind.

I liken this congestion zone within a triangle to an ever-tightening coiled spring until the energy is suddenly released and the market breaks out of the formation with strong and often violent moves.

I like to search out those triangles that are a long time in forming because they normally can be relied upon to give me a trade that is not only quickly in profit from the outset, but usually results in a very large move. It is near the top of my list for trading setups.

Figure 1.3.9 shows two triangles in the hourly Apple chart.

The first triangle here is long in its formation and completes in around six weeks and so I could forecast that the move out was likely to be explosive. It certainly was! Apple gained $50 – or around 10% – in just a few days. The second triangle is shorter but the move down out of it was so strong, it created a large gap. That was a signal that a strong down move lay ahead.

FIGURE 1.3.9

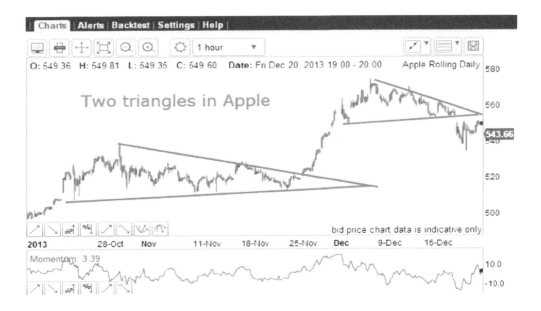

A good visual sense is helpful. If you have a good visual sense, you should have little difficulty picking up triangles that are about to complete. Of course, when in their early stages of development, they are indistinguishable from normal market noise. It is only in their latter stages of formation that they become recognisable, when there are several touch points on each line. But the earlier you can place your lines, the more prepared you will be for correctly trading this pattern.

Figure 1.3.10 shows a small triangle working in the hourly USD/JPY. I have annotated the chart to show how I would trade this pattern.

The market had been moving up in a long run to early January and had entered a period of consolidation. Recent action shows a clear triangle and a likely upside breakout where I went long. Incidentally, I could possibly have waited for a break above the high point of the triangle. That would be a more conservative policy. I entered my protective stop just under the recent lows of the triangle for a very manageable 25 pip risk.

How many touch points are needed to validate a triangle?

I like to see at least three touch points on both the lower and higher lines to validate the triangle. Fewer touch points would cause me to question the pattern.

FIGURE 1.3.10

Trading the wedge

This is one of my favourite patterns. It's a slight variation on the triangle and is most often a **reversal pattern**. It consists of converging lines of support and resistance, **but both in the same direction**, either both sloping up or sloping down. When you spot one on the daily or weekly chart, the move out of it is usually spectacular. They almost always resolve in the direction opposite to their slope.

A great example in the Dow is shown in Figure 1.3.11.

On this hourly chart, the market was in rally mode with the lines of support (lower) and resistance (upper) converging. Something had to give! And on 29 November, the lower line suffered a small break. This was the time to enter a short order just below the lower line, looking for a more substantial break.

FIGURE 1.3.11

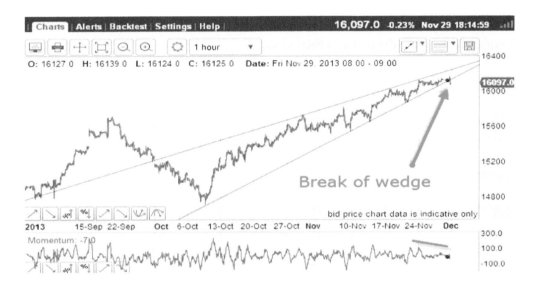

How did that trade develop? Let's look at Figure 1.3.12.

FIGURE 1.3.12

The market broke sharply lower and a low-risk short trade was on. The protective stop was placed just above the late November high for a low-risk trade. A possible gain of 300 to 400 pips was available.

I explain how I trade the wedge in Section 3.4.

3. The Five-Wave Continuation

This is a pattern that I first discovered a few years ago. It can occur during a major trend and signifies a **continuation** of the trend. Figure 1.3.13 shows an example in GBP/USD.

FIGURE 1.3.13

The trend has started down and I have four complete waves with the market starting the fifth wave down. Confirmation of the pattern will occur when the market breaks the w3 low. Until then, we do not have a confirmed pattern. In fact, we may have an A-B-C down to the marked w3, leading to a rally phase.

How can I identify this pattern?

There are two rules for this pattern:

Rule 1: The w4 must overlap w1 and w3 must go beyond w1.

This makes it a different animal to the impulsive Elliott Wave five-wave pattern, which requires non-overlap of waves 4 and 1. If w4 does not overlap w1, then you do not have a genuine continuation pattern.

Rule 2: The big difference to keep in mind is the fifth wave of a five-wave impulse Elliott Wave pattern is a terminating wave to be followed by a counter-trend move. The fifth wave of my five-wave continuation pattern is a continuation wave. In the latter, you are looking for w5 to continue the main trend.

Also, the waves 2, 3 and 4 should be of roughly the same time duration.

Figure 1.3.14 shows a confirmed pattern in USD/CAD.

FIGURE 1.3.14

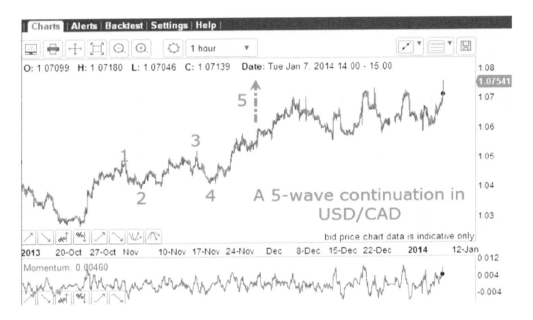

From the late October low, the market started up and made a lovely five-wave pattern with the fifth wave confirmed when the market broke above the w3 high in late November. That was a signal to trade from the long side.

How can I trade this pattern?

Probably the most reliable way to trade these patterns is to wait for the w4 to be put in, ensure it overlaps w1, and then enter a stop entry order beyond the extent of w3.

With experience, it becomes possible to anticipate the w5 move as w4 is being put in.

4. The Key Reversal

This is a quite rare pattern that I use only when it appears on the daily, weekly or monthly charts and when it occurs at the end of a strong trending market. When it does occur, it can lead to a violent trend reversal that takes most by surprise and is well worth trading.

It consists of a move first in the direction of the established trend to make a new high/low. Then, during the day/week/month, the market moves against that trend and closes higher/lower than the previous period. In a bear market on the daily, it makes a new low during the day but recovers and closes higher than the previous day's close.

A terrific example in the US Dollar Index is shown in Figure 1.3.15, which is on the hourly chart for clarity.

FIGURE 1.3.15

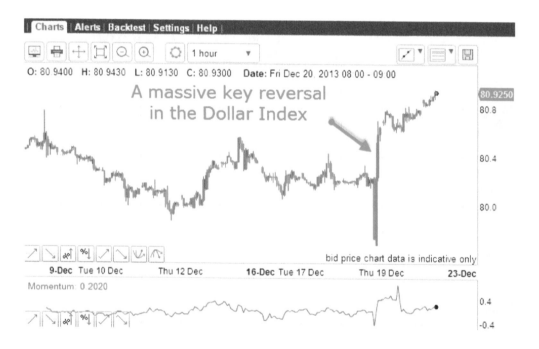

The market had been falling for some time and on 18 December, it moved well below the 80 level where many sell-stops had been placed. When these were satisfied, the buying took over and the market zoomed upwards as there were few sellers remaining after the wash-out earlier. This is a sign of selling **exhaustion** and is very often the prelude to a vigorous new trend, as here.

If you were not aware that this is a key reversal, you could be whipsawed; first by going long on the 12 to 14 December rally ("is the low finally in here?") and being stopped out on the break of the 80 level for a loss. You might then be tempted to go short on this break as it appeared the down trend had been re-established. This short trade would again produce a loss on the rally. That is a classic whipsaw!

We all have been victims, but if you can put your annoyance to one side and view the market objectively, you would immediately go long, having correctly appraised the trend had likely changed to up.

How did this trade develop? Let's look at Figure 1.3.16.

FIGURE 1.3.16

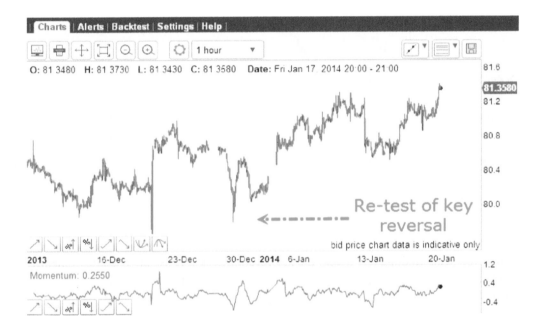

There was a typical re-test of the low, but when it held, it was up and away. If you had a long trade stopped out on this re-test, there was another long signal given when the market gapped up on 2 January.

Another example in the weekly chart of the Nikkei is shown in Figure 1.3.17.

The Nikkei had been in a solid, strong rally since October with only two lower weekly closes! That was some one-way rally. But no market climbs forever and the rally ended with an explosive blow-off exhaustion climax and the weekly bar shows a new high near the 16,000 level and then dropping sharply to close much lower than the previous week. That changed the trend for a few weeks before buying emerged to re-establish the uptrend.

There was ample opportunity to take large profits from the down move (as well as from the rally phase).

FIGURE 1.3.17

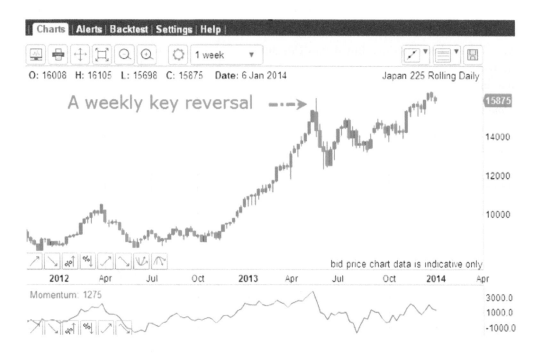

Naturally, a key reversal signal on the weekly chart is too coarse a scale for timing precise entries for swing trading, but within the key reversal week it is usually possible to identify the trend change on the daily or even the hourly chart. By Thursday or Friday of the week in question, it is usually possible to anticipate a weekly key reversal.

Figure 1.3.18 shows the famous top in gold in 2011 on the daily chart.

Gold had been in an historic multi-year bull market but it finally came to an end at the double tops in late 2011 where there are two daily key reversals. On each day, the market had made a new high but closed lower on the day. The second top was the final buying climax and it was downhill from then on.

The key reversal is a more accurate indication of a trend change when it comes after an extended run. I rarely find it a useful trade signal on a chart time frame of less than daily. With candlesticks they stand out as either a red bar (for a buying climax) or a green bar (for a selling climax).

FIGURE 1.3.18

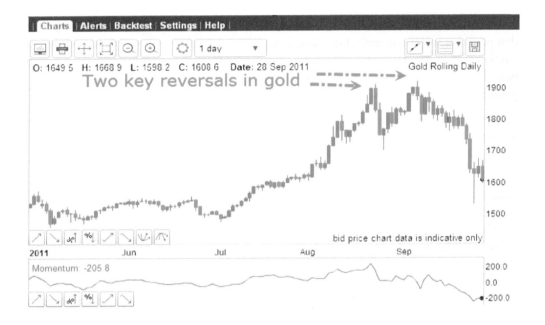

Summary

I have four favourite chart patterns:

1. Head & Shoulders (reversal)

2. Triangles and Wedges (continuation or reversal, depending on context)

3. The Five-Wave Continuation

4. The Key Reversal (reversal)

The true H&S is quite rare, but Triangles are very common. The Five-Wave Continuation is fairly common, but the Key Reversal is rare, especially on the weekly and monthly charts.

It is the Triangle (and Wedge) that offer the most trading opportunities.

1.4 Momentum

The momentum indicator is one of the first technical tools ever developed and it is the only one I use. It simply adds up a series of the closing prices in a given time frame for the most recent number of periods and then averages that sum. For instance, the 12-hour momentum reading is the average closing price for the previous 12 one-hour periods. The 12-day momentum is the average closing price for the previous 12 days.

The 12-period momentum is the standard given in your trading platform. You can change that period at will if you wish. But using a shorter span (say five periods) would produce a wildly swinging pattern which would be unusable. Using a much longer span (say 50 periods) would give you a very flat read-out which is also unusable. I have found the 12-period is a satisfactory compromise.

As markets rally, the momentum generally rises and *vice versa*. Thus in a rally phase I do not need the momentum to tell me the market is going up – I can see that from the price action alone!

> The only time I watch momentum closely is when I expect a market turn, where I am looking for a *divergence with price*.

Why is a momentum divergence event important?

A divergence is simply when the momentum fails to match the price. An example on the hourly chart of gold is provided in Figure 1.4.1.

FIGURE 1.4.1

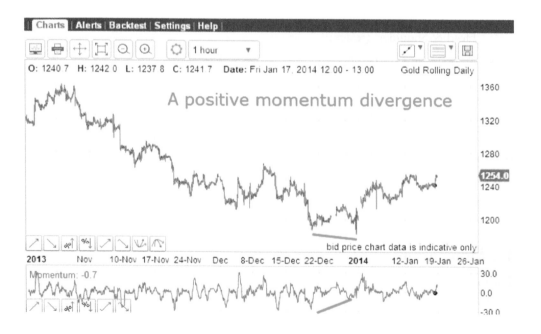

The market was in a solid down trend since October but in December, the market made another low on the 31st, *but the momentum did not* as it failed to follow the price to a new low. This usually is an indication that the selling power is getting weaker and to get ready for a counter-trend rally, at least. And that is what the market gave us – a rally out of a positive momentum divergence.

These are the only momentum signals I take notice of.

Can I use momentum divergences alone when looking for a change in trend?

It is not a good idea to focus on just momentum divergences. I always require other evidence, such as a complete fifth Elliott Wave, or a Fibonacci retrace, or a tramline target (or all three, ideally). Markets are littered with many false divergences where, after a relief counter-trend move, the market continues along its main trend. Therefore, momentum divergence is supplementary evidence, not full evidence on its own.

I consider a momentum divergence as additional evidence for a trend change.

Figure 1.4.2 shows an example in the daily chart of EUR/USD.

FIGURE 1.4.2

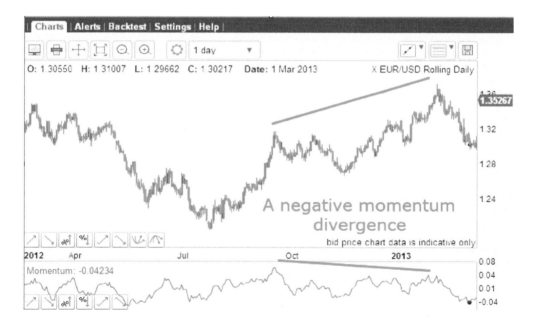

A major high was made in September and after a period of consolidation the market went on to make a new high well above the previous one, but the momentum failed to do the same. This set up the negative momentum divergence and produced the sharp declines. The entire rally was in the classic A-B-C form, which is counter-trend. This indicates a short trade was the correct stance.

The Momentum Rule

The larger the momentum divergence, the sharper the eventual reversal.

I pay no attention to momentum divergences in charts of time scales of less than one hour. When they appear on weekly, daily or hourly charts, that is the time to start taking notice.

CHAPTER 2

CHARTING WITH TRAMLINES

Viewing the markets through tramlines is a very simple but powerful way to analyse market action and provides you with high-confidence trade entries at low risk. Not only that, but tramlines offer accurate price targets. This places you in the strong position of being able to plan a trade well ahead of time, to assess your maximum risk and also project your likely profit. Many of my best trades are made with this technique as the starting point.

In this chapter I will explain how I draw tramlines and the **Tramline Trading Rule**. I then explain what is a **Prior Pivot Point** (PPP) and how it helps to validate a tramline. After finding a tramline pair, I explain how useful **third tramlines** are for fixing the important price targets following a **tramline break**. Then I show why you should look out for the **Chinese hat** and I also show how to determine sensible **protective stops** using tramlines.

So, these are the sections in this chapter:

1. Drawing tramlines and the Tramline Trading Rule

2. How to find the best tramlines

3. The Prior Pivot Point (PPP)

4. Will the market change trend at a tramline?

5. Tramline trios

6. Setting protective stops with tramlines

7. When tramlines cross over – the Chinese hat

8. Using the third tramline to set a price target

2.1 Drawing tramlines and the Tramline Trading Rule

In the first chapter I introduced the idea of trendlines (Section 1.2). Now I will show how they are the very basis of my tramline method.

I am drawing a distinction between a **trendline** and a **tramline:**

- A *trendline* is a line joining the lows in a bull market and the highs in a bear market.

- A *tramline* is a parallel line to the trendline which joins the highs in a bull market and the lows in a bear market.

This gives us a **trading channel** between the tramlines. Most trading platforms have the parallel line tool and it should be a simple task to place tramlines on any chart once you fix your trendline.

A genuine trendline joins the highs/lows with accurate touch points, but since nature does not always give us perfection, we must often make some allowance for when some of the touch points do not accurately meet your line. You must then make an attempt at a **best fit** and this often involves cutting off pigtails (as I have described earlier).

A **tramline** drawn parallel to your trendline will contain all of the trading activity between the lines – the trading channel. The upper tramline will represent **resistance** to the rallies and the lower tramline will represent **support** to the dips.

What we are looking for in a tramline (once we have a good trendline) is a best fit for the highs/lows in a given time period.

As an example, Figure 2.1.1 shows once again a chart I used in Chapter 1.

FIGURE 2.1.1

My upper line is the original trendline with four accurate touch points and a pigtail cut-off. The parallel line beneath it is my lower tramline and contains two accurate touch points and a pigtail cut-off. Except for the small overshoot near the top, all trading in this period takes place between the tramlines in the **trading channel**.

With no other chart information, we should expect trading to continue within this channel. This gives us clues as to how to trade this market.

The Tramline Trading Rule

Go short/sell longs when the market is at or near the upper tramline. This applies especially with up-sloping tramlines (bull market).

Go long/cover shorts when the market is at or near the lower tramline. This applies especially with down-sloping tramlines (bear market).

This rule aligns your trade with the main trend inside the trading channel. This is trading with the trend – the usual way to trade for the best results. I have another rule for dealing with tramline breaks (when the market breaks outside the trading channel) and I will discuss this later.

2.2 How to find the best tramlines

Sometimes, the highs and lows do not lie accurately on straight lines and you must resort to finding a best fit. In Section 1.1, I showed the following chart (Figure 2.2.1) to illustrate one problem with fixing a good trendline when the touch points do not accurately line up.

FIGURE 2.2.1

Either of the two lines drawn here could work as a trendline, but so far the one I prefer is the one with the steeper slope since it takes in the exact tip of the high and the most recent high. But the matter could be settled by finding their respective tramlines. Figure 2.2.2 shows the tramline pair using the steeper trendline.

Here on the lower tramline I have highly accurate touch points on the recent spike lows, a pigtail cut-off on the early December spike low, a small touch point near the start of the trading channel and two lovely PPPs (Prior Pivot Points, which I will cover in the next section).

In this way, I can say that the lower tramline is reliable as a line of support and my upper tramline is a reliable line of resistance.

That fact validates the upper (parallel) tramline.

If the lower tramline was not so reliable because of fewer touch points, or no PPPs, then that would invalidate the corresponding upper tramline.

FIGURE 2.2.2

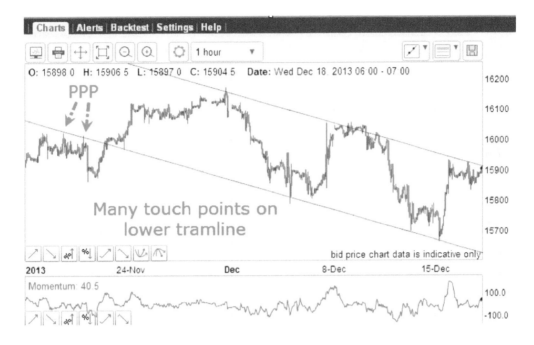

Does the alternate trendline give us as reliable a lower tramline?

Figure 2.2.3 shows the chart again but with the alternative, shallower trendline.

My corresponding lower tramline for this trendline has three accurate touch points, but there is no PPP. The line just slices through the trading before entering the trading channel with no accurate touch points. Because of this, I would put this pair in a lesser light than the first and prefer that trendline and tramline pair for trading.

> **The general rule is this**: the more accurate touch points on both tramlines and a good PPP on one of them means you have a reliable tramline pair. Missing any one of these and you can place less confidence in the tramlines.

There are two setups with tramlines where you have a tradable event: continuation of the trend at a tramline and trend reversal at a tramline break. I will cover this in Section 2.4, but first, I must explain what is a Prior Pivot Point and why it is an important feature of tramlines.

FIGURE 2.2.3

2.3 The Prior Pivot Point (PPP)

When the market has entered into the trading channel between the tramline pair, the two lines are the boundaries that the market respects (until we get a tramline break, of course). I have found a curious phenomenon in many tramline setups. Just before the market enters into this channel, it makes a kiss on one of the tramlines as if to recognise it as a valid line of support/resistance.

Figure 2.3.1 – a Dow hourly chart – illustrates what I mean.

My lower tramline on the Dow hourly chart has multiple touch points and is reliable. I draw my upper tramline through the one major high. Just before the trading channel was entered on the sharp decline, the market ran across the top of this line because it was then acting as support. But after the break into the channel, it reversed role and acted as resistance.

The line was transformed from a support line to a resistance line at the break.

This is a key concept.

FIGURE 2.3.1

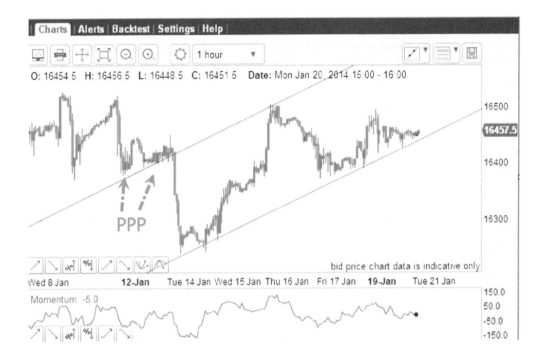

I call the touches on the support part of the line **Prior Pivot Points (PPP)**. They can be close to the break or distant. If they appear far away, they gain in importance.

My PPP Rule

When I have a good accurate PPP, my confidence in that tramline increases greatly.

If I do not have a PPP on either tramline, then I generally look for another tramline pair. Sometimes, I just have to give up on finding a good tramline pair until there is more chart development. In this case, I simply go to the charts on other markets that do give me tramlines rich in PPPs. These will most often provide better trading setups anyway. Concentrate on the best setups and ignore the questionable ones.

Incidentally, I have coined the term *Prior Pivot Point* in recognition that there is a well-established meaning for the term *pivot point* in technical analysis (as well as my use of the term for drawing Fibonacci levels – see Section 3.7). This is a totally different concept and the two should not be confused.

2.4 Will the market change trend at a tramline?

When the market is in the trading channel and closely approaching one of the tramlines, it has two options: either it will bounce off the tramline in a continuation of the main trend, or it will break the tramline in a trend reversal. Obviously, the implications for any trade you make here are polar opposites. For example, if you are trading for a bounce off the tramline and the market breaks through it, you will be in a losing trade.

Continuation of the trend at a tramline

If you have no reason to suspect the trend is about to change (from Elliott Waves or Fibonacci retraces), then you will be looking to go long on a lower tramline in a bull market. The closer the market approaches your tramline, the lower the risk of the trade you are planning. This is because your protective stop is typically placed just underneath the tramline, close to your entry. This is the ideal situation.

But, in practice, the market often hovers just above the tramline several tens of pips away.

Do you just take the trade in anticipation that the market may not touch the line accurately before moving higher with the trend?

That is one of the toughest problems associated with tramline trading! And there is no easy answer. If you wait for an exact hit and it fails to make it, you may miss a great trade. If so, then take comfort from not losing any money and move on. Decisions like this must be individual to you and fit in with your risk profile.

I should mention one other problem – when you get a **head fake**. This is when the tramline is broken momentarily, and then shoots back into the trading channel. If you have your protective stop hit, you will have to take the loss and see the market validate your analysis – a double whammy. This could make you feel annoyed and determined to get even with the market. But this attitude could be a big mistake. It is an example of emotional trading, which should be avoided (see my Eleven Commandments at the end of the text).

Probably the best policy then is to just keep monitoring that setup because that head fake may be a sign that the market really does want to turn and it could give you a good trade signal later.

Trend change at a tramline break

When a tramline is broken decisively, that means the near-term trend has changed (and possibly the longer-term trend likewise). But this may or may not develop into a major new trend – the future price action will determine that. At least if you can get on board a new trend early at a tramline break that will give you a head start over most other traders who remain with the old trend and are seeing their profits vanish.

I love to trade tramline breaks because if the new trend does develop into something substantial I am on board early and can afford to ride the small counter-trend moves. A trader getting in later has a much higher risk and may be stopped out on one of these reversals.

A great example in gold is shown in Figure 2.4.1.

FIGURE 2.4.1

My upper tramline has multiple touch points and so can be considered reliable. A long trade was signalled on the break. At the current market, there is a $40 gain in this trade and we could be at the start of a major move – time will tell. But the tramline break signal has enabled me to get on board this potential bull move early. And because most traders were expecting the market to continue falling into January, many will be suspicious of the rally and will want to see if the market can maintain it before making a long trade commitment.

It is these Johnnies-come-lately that drive the market into its final push before reversing. If you understand this is how the markets work, you can take money off these latecomers by trading against them. You will be taking profits while they will be entering a risky trade.

2.5 Tramline trios

Once you have a reliable tramline pair, you can draw at once the third tramline when one of the original tramlines is broken. You will need to place it by eye and so absolute accuracy is not possible. But you should be able to do a good job by holding a ruler up to the chart on your screen (which you can maximise). This way, you can measure your line separations quite accurately.

Here is the hourly gold chart again in Figure 2.5.1.

FIGURE 2.5.1

From the initial tramline break, the market has moved up to the third tramline, backed away as it respected the resistance, and then pushed on up through the line. It then backed down to the line, **which is now support** because of the earlier break. When you took the long trade on the tramline break in the $1,220 area, you could immediately set your target at the third tramline. Naturally, because at this stage you do not know the precise price level where on the third tramline the market will hopefully hit, you will need to monitor the rally's progress.

You can then enter a limit order at your target in case you are away from your screen when the event occurs. Remember, we see a lot of rapid spike moves in gold and a limit order will guarantee you a fill if the market moves through your price. Of course, you will need to enter your protective stop as quickly as possible, or better yet, do that at the same time as you place your initial order.

Naturally, because the tramline slopes down, you are hoping for a rapid ascent to the line since that would give you the maximum profit. A more leisurely rally would produce a lower value for the hit. The market did hit the third tramline in the $1254 area for a nice $34 profit in a little less than two weeks, making it a typical swing trade for profit and duration.

Sometimes, it is possible to draw fourth and even fifth tramlines, which are useful in a very trending market. These will often give you intermediate targets and areas where the market may at least consolidate for a while.

2.6 Setting protective stops with tramlines

Once you have a reliable tramline pair in place, setting stops can be straightforward, especially if there are some recent minor highs/lows nearby.

I will illustrate this in the Dow chart shown in Figure 2.6.1.

FIGURE 2.6.1

I have taken a long trade on the lower tramline at the 16,400 level in accordance to my Tramline Trading Rule.

Where to place the protective stop?

The touch points prior to my entry form a minor low on the move down off the upper tramline touch point in a kind of "V" pattern. I believe a move down under the apex of the "V" would indicate a decisive tramline break and my protective stop placed here would be sensible. That indicates a maximum potential risk of around 40 pips. This is a typical risk when I trade the Dow.

Ideally, the market would advance to the upper tramline – perhaps to the 16,700 level or above. That would give a potential reward/risk ratio of a very acceptable seven-to-one.

Here, I am trading with the trend (up), taking a long position near the lower tramline and setting a protective stop far enough away from the tramline to avoid most head fakes. My maximum risk is 40 pips, which is within my risk tolerance. And I have a target at the upper tramline.

In summary, this is a logical trade complete with risk management and a target for my exit. If you follow this procedure on every trade, you have a total trading method.

What do you do when there is no minor high/low nearby?

That is a great question. Figure 2.6.2 is an example in a bear market in the daily EUR/GBP.

FIGURE 2.6.2

I have a terrific lower tramline anchored by three PPPs (with two excellent early ones far away from the trading channel), and my upper tramline takes in the two major highs to late October. In early November, the market made a hit on the tramline and a high-probability short trade could be entered there. But where to place your protective stop, since there are no minor highs in the vicinity?

The only recourse is to use a *money stop*, which is to assign your usual risk (say 50 pips). That's about all you can do and it is usually satisfactory. If the market rallies by 50 pips above your entry, that would likely indicate a tramline break and a change of trend. You do not want to be short in a bull market!

2.7 When tramlines cross over – the Chinese hat

We often meet a situation where we have a long-term tramline pair working in the direction of the major trend and also a shorter-term tramline pair along a counter-trend move. Where they meet and cross over, I call that a **Chinese hat** because of the similarity of shapes.

Figure 2.7.1 is the hourly Dow chart where the longer-term upper down-sloping tramline pair intersects the short-term up-sloping tramline pair. At point **a** two upper tramlines meet and because upper tramlines are always lines of resistance, the cross-over is an area of extra-strong resistance. That is why the market was sent back down hard when it reached that point.

But the interesting hat is the point **b** where both tramlines represent extra-strong support. The long-term upper tramline was broken and now the market is attempting a kiss on to what is now support. If this double support gives way, we will have both a kiss failure and a lower tramline break, which is potentially very bearish.

FIGURE 2.7.1

One way to trade these hats is as if they will hold the market and can thus place a close stop for a low-risk trade. But if I am stopped out trading the 'b' hat (where in the example in Figure 2.7.1 I would be long), I would reverse my position and end up net short.

Breaking through a hat takes a lot of buying/selling power, so a break is a very significant event. Usually, the market moves swiftly after a hat break as many sell stops are hit. Figure 2.7.2 shows the chart just a few moments later.

FIGURE 2.7.2

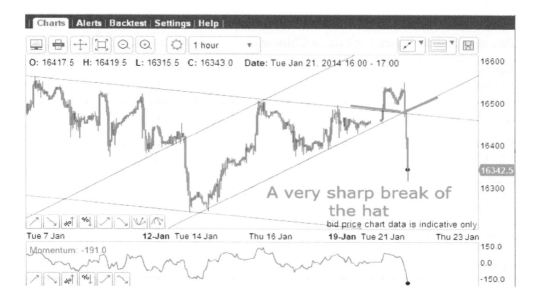

That is one sharp move following the hat break! Do you see the potential for trading the hats in your charts? A great way to play the Chinese hat is to assume it will break and place an entry stop order just a little away from the hat. If you get the break, you will be in at a great price. If not, then no harm is done.

2.8 Using the third tramline to set a price target

The third tramline often gives you a very accurate price target following a tramline break. I recommend always drawing in the third tramline whenever you have a tramline break.

Using the example in the Dow from Section 2.7, Figure 2.8.1 shows the same chart just a few moments later.

Despite the market being in freefall, it knew when to stop falling – right on the third tramline. And the market has made a large bounce from this level. Isn't that impressive? A nimble trader could have gained around 150 pips in an hour or so on this trade, which was made possible from a basic knowledge of tramlines and their targets.

Naturally, with sloping tramlines, a third tramline target is a moveable feast. But you should be able to make a sensible estimate of your likely target in most cases. The alternative is to watch the market throughout the day and be ready to exit the trade as the third tramline is approached.

FIGURE 2.8.1

Summary

1. I have shown how to draw tramlines to get the best fit, how to look for PPPs and how the Tramline Trading Rule works, along with stop placement rules.

2. Then, I have used reliable tramlines to give me high-confidence, low-risk trade entries and how to set price targets using the third tramline.

3. I have also described the Chinese hat and shown how such a powerful pattern can be recognised and exploited.

4. Finally, I would just say that using my system you do not need to look in exotic markets for great trades. There are usually plenty of setups in a week in just a few major markets. If you have limited time to devote to trading, the fewer markets you follow, the better your results will be. Hone your skills on just a few markets – I suggest the Dow, EUR/USD and gold as your core markets.

Part 2

How To Trade The Tramline Method

CHAPTER 3

TRADING WITH TRAMLINES, FIBONACCI AND ELLIOTT WAVES

In this chapter, I show how I go about trading the various patterns that I have described. When researching a possible trade, I go through these five steps:

My Five-Step Trading Routine

1. Recognise the pattern and put it in context.

2. Work out a trading plan with entry price, risk level to stop and profit targets.

3. Wait for confirmation of the pattern.

4. Then place the trade and protective stop.

5. Finally, manage the trade to completion.

I recommend you to implement this routine on every trade you make. It will hopefully prevent you from making that rash trade ever again!

In this chapter I will cover:

1. The Tramline Trading Rules

2. Trading the tramline break

3. Trading the head fake

4. Trading the wedge

5. Trading the "V"

6. Trading the kiss and scalded cat bounce

7. How to use Fibonacci levels

8. Using basic Elliott Wave Theory concepts

9. Context is key

3.1 The Tramline Trading Rules

In Chapter 2, I showed how to find good tramlines on almost any chart and to expect to find more than one valid set to be operating at any time. Remember, the lower tramline of a pair is a line of **support**. The upper tramline of a pair is a line of **resistance**. Here are the guidelines I use to fix on a valid tramline pair.

My guidelines for finding good tramlines

- At least one of the pair should have a PPP (Prior Pivot Point).

- At least one of the lines should have at least three accurate touch points.

- Pigtail cut-offs are allowed (but not too many).

- All trading in the period in question must be contained within the trading channel between the tramlines.

- When the market breaks through one of the tramlines, you can immediately draw in the third tramline equidistant.

Once I have confidence in my tramlines, I can apply my Trading Rules.

The Tramline Trading Rules

- In a bull market (rising tramlines) the general rule is to go long/cover shorts at or near the lower tramline.

- In a bull market with a tramline trio, the centre tramline (which was support) now becomes resistance when it is broken. If the market rallies to this line in a kiss, that kiss offers a new short-selling opportunity.

- In a bear market (falling tramlines) the general rule is to sell longs/go short at or near the upper tramline.

- In a bear market with a tramline trio, the centre tramline (which was resistance) now becomes support when it is broken. If the market declines to this line in a kiss, that kiss offers a new long opportunity.

A good example in AUD/NZD is shown in Figure 3.1.1.

FIGURE 3.1.1

The market is in a solid downtrend and has just rallied to the upper tramline. This is where a short trade is indicated with a protective stop just above the line for a low-risk trade.

The target is now the lower tramline and if it reaches it, the profit can be taken. But what if the tramline is broken to the upside?

Let's move on to trading the tramline break.

3.2 Trading the tramline break

Tramlines do not work forever. At some point the market will break through one of them and when I see a tramline break I get excited by the potential whale trade that lies ahead. That is because a genuine break signals to me that the trend has very likely changed and I stand a good chance of being on board the new trend right from the very start, well before most traders have realised what has happened. Most of my best trades have started from a tramline break.

The other advantage is this: when I have a good position early in the new trend, I can afford to let minor set-backs run their course with little effect on my stress levels. If you jump on board a well-developed trend, there is every chance you will be caught up in a big counter-trend move, putting your position under water – and yourself under stress.

Obviously, there is a safe limit as to how early you can determine a trend change and take a position. Get in too early and you run the considerable risk that the trend really has not changed at all. Get in too late and you may be in at near the end.

That is why my tramline method is an excellent compromise and balances the risks well.

Let's look at the Nikkei chart in Figure 3.2.1.

This is the daily Nikkei and I have a good tramline pair working, especially in the most recent period, with good touch points on my lower tramline. On 23/24 January, the market broke below the lower tramline and the sell signal was generated on the tramline break, as well as the break of the most recent low touch point.

In addition, there was a negative momentum divergence at the recent high on the upper tramline, indicating likely buying exhaustion.

The break has signalled a change in trend and until otherwise disproved, trading from the short side is indicated.

FIGURE 3.2.1

Let's now look at Figure 3.2.2, which shows the situation developing.

FIGURE 3.2.2

If I draw in the third (lower) tramline, the market is currently testing this line of support and a short-term profit can be taken. Only a move above the centre tramline would indicate the new downtrend was not established yet. Provided the centre tramline operates as a solid line of resistance, the trend is now down.

Figure 3.2.3 shows a terrific example of a clean tramline break in USD/CAD.

FIGURE 3.2.3

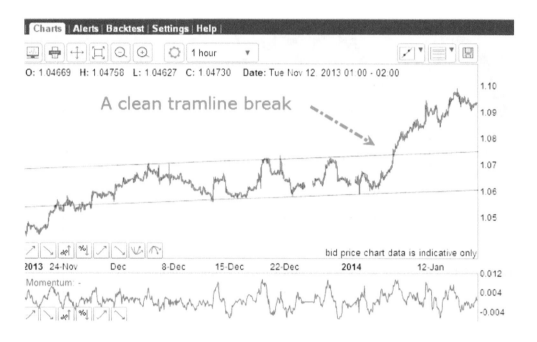

The buy signal was given when the market moved up out of the trading channel and above the previous highs. Using the simple strategy of placing a buy-stop entry just above the upper tramline would have got you into a terrific trade.

How can I play a possible tramline break when I already have a position?

This is where a very useful strategy can be deployed. Referring to Figure 3.2.4, let's say you are short AUD/NZD from November.

At the end of January you see the market is testing the centre tramline and decide to exit your trade if it breaks above it. A few days later, the tramline suffered an upside break. If you had entered your protect-profit stop just above the now centre line, that order could have been a **stop-and-reverse order** where you would be taken out of your short trade and immediately go long **at the same price**. It simply involves entering a buy-stop order for twice the size of your original short trade.

FIGURE 3.2.4

Where is the first target for the new long trade?

The first target for the new long trade is at the third tramline – which you have immediately drawn in, of course. And the market is currently testing the resistance at this new line.

Because the downtrend was getting long in the tooth in the first chart, you would naturally suspect that the inevitable tramline break would occur sooner rather than later. This observation would encourage you to employ the stop-and-reverse strategy.

It is possible that the market will now decline to kiss the centre tramline. Time will tell.

3.3 Trading the head fake

A head fake is an annoying fact of life. Just when we believe we have identified a great tramline break and the market is going in our direction, it suddenly decides it wants to turn back on you and trade again inside the trading channel. Meanwhile, your trade which was nicely in profit is now under water and you are in danger of being stopped out.

What to do?

Naturally, the disciplined course of action is – inaction. Let the market take you out if that is what it wants to do. You determined your stop level rationally before you placed the trade and you are wrong. But your loss is within the risk limits you have set, so be glad the loss is small!

Put that trade behind you and keep looking at this market because the head fake may be trying to tell you something to your advantage. Don't make the common mistake of walking away from that market in disgust muttering "the system doesn't work."

A particularly nasty example of a head fake is shown in Figure 3.3.1.

FIGURE 3.3.1

I have a superb tramline pair working and on 15 January I had the tramline break I was looking for. That gave me a fill on my short trade at the 1.6345 level and my protective stop was placed at 1.6400, just inside the trading channel.

The market ran down to the 1.6320 level, giving me a small gain, but then turned tail and quickly ran up back above the tramline and I was stopped out for a 55 pip loss.

Should I abandon trading this market or keep searching?

I noted that the rally back inside the trading channel was very sharp and that gave me the idea that we had a false tramline break and the market really wanted to move higher. I then decided to look for a long trade and the result is shown in Figure 3.3.2.

The reversal back up was sharp and the market entered the trading channel and then backed and filled before making a decisive move above that consolidation area – and that gave me a buy signal where I had placed a buy stop order. If the market had moved down instead of up here, that would have given me a sell signal. In that case, we would have had another tramline break and I could trade it as usual.

FIGURE 3.3.2

The subsequent rally towards the upper tramline was also sharp and a 200-pip profit was available on that trade, which more than made up for the original loss.

Just reading what the market was telling me was the key factor. I did not have any pre-conceptions of what the market ought to do. I simply let it speak and acted in accordance with its messages.

So the head fake was not so disastrous after all!

3.4 Trading the wedge

I like the wedge! It is a very reliable chart pattern that warns of an impending trend change if it occurs near the end of a long trend. Some traders call it an ascending/descending triangle or an ending diagonal. It is formed from a pattern where the support and resistance lines converge and travel in the same direction. These end-of-trend patterns do not come along every day, though. But when they do, I like to take the trades very seriously.

Let's look at a fabulous long-term example in Alcoa, which I had been tracking since making its low in 2012. My interest was sparked by the divergence of the main US stock averages, which were in strong rally mode, to that of Alcoa, which had fallen from a high near $50 in 2007 to the $6 area in the same period. Intriguingly, Alcoa was one of the 30 components of the Dow Jones Industrials (until demoted in 2013) and is traded on high volumes.

Naturally, there were good reasons for the decline: aluminium was in over-supply and its price was dropping along with a general decline in the commodity sector. At one point I noted that Alcoa was the most heavily shorted stock in the DJIA. If the market could rally off a base, a good short squeeze could develop. And since late 2011, it looked to me as if it was forming such a base.

Figure 3.4.1 shows the picture in October 2013 on the daily chart.

FIGURE 3.4.1

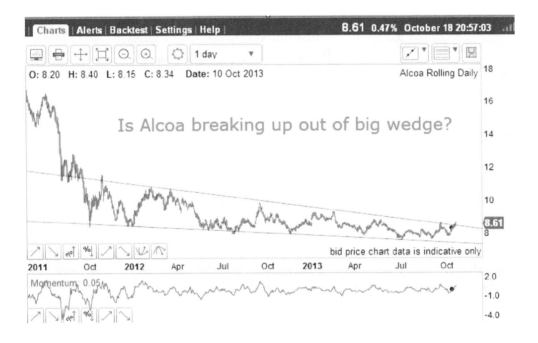

The market had been trading between the support and resistance lines of my large, multi-month wedge. Remember, this came after the market had suffered a large trending decline off the $50 area, which made the wedge noteworthy as a possible signal to get ready to cover shorts and go long if the wedge was an ending pattern, as seemed highly likely.

Naturally, the touch points are not all perfectly accurate, but there are enough hits and near-misses to give me high confidence that if the market could break up from this formation, the move should be sharp and strong.

The updated chart from three months later is shown in Figure 3.4.2.

As expected, the upward break was sharp and now the uptrend slope is much sharper than the downside moves within the wedge. This has all the hallmarks of a major trend change.

FIGURE 3.4.2

When you have identified a wedge at the end of a long downtrend, what is the best way to play it?

I like to place entry buy stops just above the most recent significant high and just above the down-sloping line. On the top chart (Figure 3.4.1), there was just such a high in the 8.60 area.

Another example in the Dow on the hourly chart is shown in Figure 3.4.3.

I was looking for a top since momentum was waning and I could count five waves in the latest rally leg. Also, the wedge pattern appeared after a long bull run. My lower wedge line has several accurate touch points, which meant that I could rely on it as a solid line of support and a break of it would likely signal a trend change – at least on the hourly chart. I reckoned that a break of this line should signal at least a temporary change of trend. There should be at least 200-300 pips in a short trade since that would be a 50% retrace of the leg up – a common retrace level.

FIGURE 3.4.3

Figure 3.4.4 shows how the trade developed.

FIGURE 3.4.4

As I suspected, the break of the wedge produced a sharp decline to give an approximate 300 pip gain which could have been taken since the market had fallen into chart support and a Fibonacci 50% correction.

Of course, a trader may have been looking for a major trend change here, but I am a relatively conservative trader and will take that profit on at least part of my position. For short-term trading, the most advantageous attitude is to enter a short trade on high bullishness and exit it on high bearishness.

Figure 3.4.5 shows another example on the 15-min chart of EUR/USD.

FIGURE 3.4.5

I have three very accurate touch points on my upper wedge line (resistance) and three touch points on my lower wedge line. But with only three widely-spaced touch points on this lower line, I am unable to place high confidence that I have a wedge working. In any case, the pattern does not appear after a long trending move.

I will pass on this as it does not qualify as a potential wedge trade.

But a great workable example in USD/JPY is shown in Figure 3.4.6.

The market had been rallying persistently from the 98 area and this wedge came at the end of a long run. I am able to draw some excellent wedge lines that contain multiple accurate touch points. The lower wedge line break was followed by a rally to kiss the underside of the line and then a **scalded cat bounce** away in a sharp move down (see Sections 3.2 and 3 6).

FIGURE 3.4.6

This was a textbook pattern; the tramline break, the kiss and then the rapid scalded cat move down. The kiss afforded an excellent opportunity to take profits on long positions and to reverse and position short using the high as a guide for the protective stop.

Now why was I looking for a top around here?

This was because I had seen a potentially complete five-wave pattern on the daily. And when I see a five-wave impulse pattern, I start looking for the turn.

Now let's look at Figure 3.4.7.

Again, this is an absolute textbook impulse wave pattern with a long and strong w3, a complex corrective w4 and a new high in w5 on a negative momentum divergence with that at the w3 high.

Not only that, but the long trade has become manically crowded with hedgies holding 158,000 short contracts and a measly 14,000 long contracts (this is information provided by the COT data at **cftc.gov** – see the Resources section at the end of the book). This is a ratio of 11/1 – a mammoth imbalance to the short side. Naturally, the smart money (the commercials) is on the other side of the trade. The potential for a massive collapse is high, once sentiment shifts. The profit potential trading against the other specs is huge.

FIGURE 3.4.7

At the very least, when the market turns, it should decline to the w4 low in the 98 area. A short trade in the 105 area with a 60 pip stop and a possible 7000 pip gain gives a potential reward/risk ratio of almost 12/1 – a most juicy prospect.

Figure 3.4.8 shows the daily GBP/USD chart with the terrific multi-month wedge forming.

My upper wedge line has at least five accurate touch points and the lower line has three. These are very reliable lines of resistance and support. Because up-sloping wedges almost always resolve in a downward break, I expect the lower line to give way and my stance will be to enter sell-stop orders just under this line.

With the momentum losing strength in the latter section of the rally, odds favour a break very soon.

This is an interesting forecast, since it flies in the face of conventional analysis. This is a common position for me to be in. In recent days, we have seen a barrage of excellent economic news for the UK from record car production to an IMF forecast for GDP to grow from 1.9% to 2.4% (a whopping increase), placing the UK as the fastest-growing economy in Western Europe. Also, with inflation having run well above the desired 2% target that the bank of England had set, the latest data show a falling rate of inflation close to the target.

On paper, GBP should be preparing for a rally continuation. But my reading of the charts says otherwise.

FIGURE 3.4.8

The minimum target for a break of a wedge is the start of it: in this case the July low at the 1.50 level.

> **My Wedge Trading Rule**
>
> An up-sloping wedge in a bull market is a terminating pattern and should be traded from the short side, looking for a move at least to the start of the wedge pattern. The opposite applies for a down-sloping wedge in a bear market.

3.5 Trading the "V"

The "V" is a small pattern that appears often at the end of a long trending run, in both the bull and bear directions. I use it to guide my entry stop orders. When the apex of the "V" is breached, that is a signal I look for to indicate a change of trend, but only when I have clues from other indicators.

The "V" starts from the high/low, then retraces to a minor low/high and then moves back to the area of the high/low where it turns again and moves back in the direction of the apex and breaks it.

As a trend progresses, I am always on the lookout for a turn to exit trending positions and to possibly reverse. My very simple rule is to place entry buy-stops (if looking for a rally) or sell-stops (if looking for a decline) just beyond the apex.

It is a technique I use frequently and its major benefit is that it enables me to exit a trending position very near the end and extract maximum profit. And if I reverse my stance, it can get me into a high reward/low risk trade near the start of the new trend. It is about as perfect and elegantly simple a trade entry/exit method as I can think of.

Figure 3.5.1 shows a great example in USD/JPY. This market had been in a solid rally phase for some weeks and I was looking for a top.

FIGURE 3.5.1

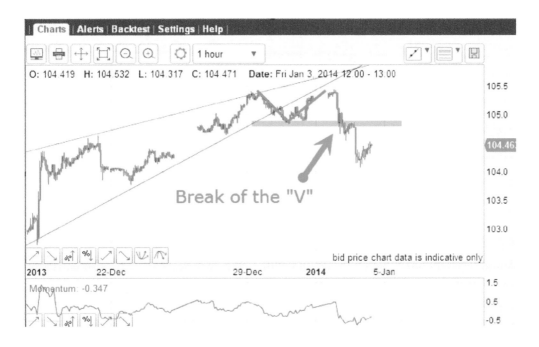

The top pattern is a "V" which I have marked out. A sell stop placed under the apex of the "V" would catch the break that was indicated by the wedge line break. So I had two solid reasons to trade it from the short side.

This is an excellent technique for judging trade entries ahead of time and also setting your protective stop. While the market was kissing the wedge line, you have plenty of time to anticipate the break of the "V", set your entry stops and when filled, enter your protective stop. If the market breaks above the wedge line and resumes its rally, nothing is lost and you would cancel your orders.

Figure 3.5.2 shows the Dow as it was making a second attempt at its all-time high on 31 December 2013 at the historic 15,600 level (see My Trading Diary in Part 3).

FIGURE 3.5.2

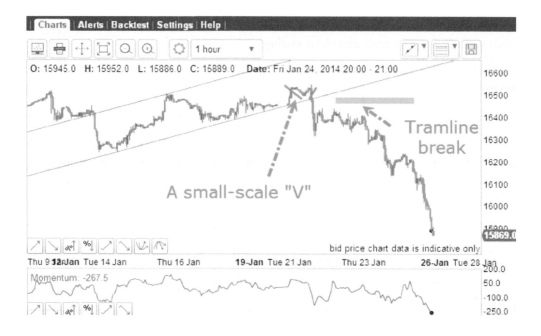

The final spurt just before the break of the lower tramline was in the shape of a "V". I have found that very often, big trends do end with a very small-scale "V" where an entry stop can be placed just under the "V" apex.

Additional encouragement for a short trade here was the breaking of the tramline, giving us two clues that the next move was likely down. As it turned out, the market entered freefall with a gain of 600 pips in just three days. This was a trade well worth stalking!

I favour this method of entry because I can place my sell-stop whenever a "V" is forming and the market is trading close to the tramline. I can do this before the downside move begins. Naturally, if I do not get a fill because the market is moving up, I can adjust my entry when I see a new "V" forming.

In general, I use the most recent high as my guide for stop-loss placement. As you can see from these two examples, the risk to the top of the "V" is very small compared with the potential gain, making it a superb low-risk trade entry method.

3.6 Trading the kiss and scalded cat bounce

When a tramline has been broken and the market has moved outside the trading channel, the market will very often come back to approach the line and make a kiss on it before saying farewell and resuming the new trend. These pullbacks can give you a great opportunity to jump on board the new trend if you missed the original trade signal at the line break.

A dramatic example in crude oil is shown in Figure 3.6.1.

FIGURE 3.6.1

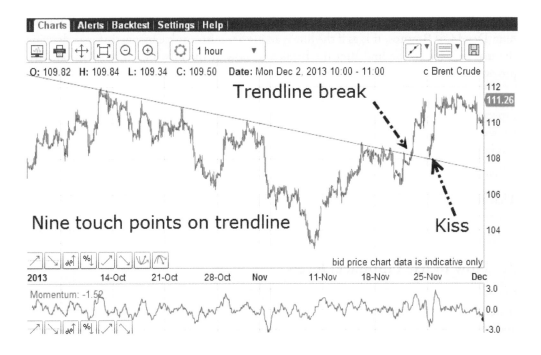

I have a superb trendline with at least nine accurate touch points. This makes it a very solid line of resistance with so many touch points. The upside break came on 21 November and the market rallied strongly. Note that the upper tramline is lengthy with many accurate touch points, which means that we can expect a mass of protective buy-stops placed above the line by those traders who have flocked to the short side along the way. These shorts have noted the strength of the resistance every time the market has rallied to it and feel confident that next time it gets near the line history will repeat.

Normally, that is the correct trading stance as the market is in a downtrend and selling at or near the trendline is a low-risk strategy. But lines of resistance do not continue forever and this large accumulation of buy-stops above the line provides the fuel for the vigorous rally following the break. Evidently, history does not repeat indefinitely.

But the market did not continue upwards immediately; instead it fell back for a **kiss** on the line.

I find that this kissing behaviour is very common and allows for a second chance to position for the change of trend. Note that the kiss was an accurate touch on the upper side of the line which was resistance before the break but is now acting as major support.

That was a second bite of the cherry to position long. Now, at the kiss, the market could have broken back underneath the line. That would have given a major failure signal – and an excellent place to enter a protective stop in case the kiss was really a brush-off! It is also an excellent place to look to position short following the failure of the line to act as support. A stop-and-reverse order could also be used (from net long to net short).

The rapid move up after the kiss I call a **Scalded Cat Bounce,** in honour of the well-known term **Dead Cat Bounce**. It is as if the line is acting as an irresistible magnetic force, drawing the market back to the line after the break and now at the kiss, in a reversal of polarity, providing an opposite force propelling the market away from the new line of support.

When you see a trendline or tramline with many accurate touch points, you can usually expect a large accumulation of stop loss orders starting at the other side of the line and a consequent sharp move covering many pips. For a quick scalp trade, these situations give excellent returns.

When you are on board such a sharp move, the question is always: where to take profits?

That is when you need to look at the larger picture; in particular, where are the chart resistance/support areas and what are the EWs telling you?

3.7 How to use Fibonacci levels

On every chart I open I am quick to apply the Fibonacci retrace levels and to keep them there. This is to give me a handy reference for likely reversals from counter-trend moves and to plan either my exit or to set up a new low-risk trade as close as possible to the appropriate level.

I always start with the most recent significant high and low. Retracements are divided into two kinds; a shallow retrace of 23% or even 38%, and a deep retrace of 62% or even 78%. The 50% level is my favourite target to aim for in most cases.

A great example in the Nasdaq is shown in Figure 3.7.1.

There is a clear move of five waves down off the 3640 high and the market is making a relief rally, as expected from Elliott Wave Theory, and the rally has carried to the 38% level where short-term profits on long trades can be taken. Hourly momentum is high and because of this odds favour at least a pause in the rally.

FIGURE 3.7.1

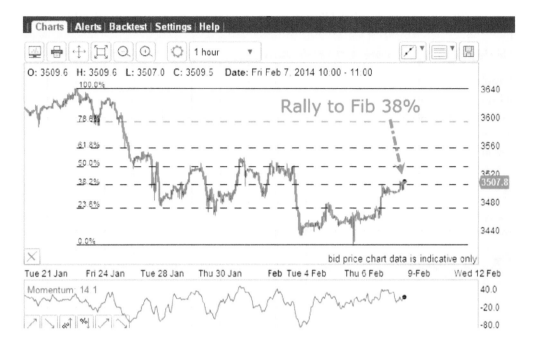

Another example in EUR/USD is shown in Figure 3.7.2.

FIGURE 3.7.2

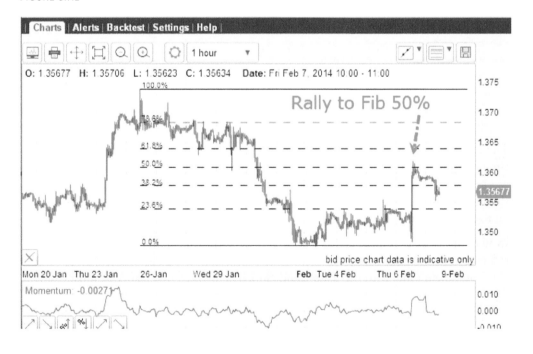

Here, the market rose very sharply to make a precise hit at the 50% level and is backing away. I am always amazed that Fibonacci levels are often as accurate as this one was at pointing out reversal areas, even in a violent market.

Do the Fibonacci levels work on the daily charts?

I apply the Fibonacci levels to the daily charts to give me likely areas for a possible trade setup. If I find the market has moved to a Fibonacci level, I then go to the hourly chart to determine a trade entry. Figure 3.7.3 is an example in AUD/USD.

FIGURE 3.7.3

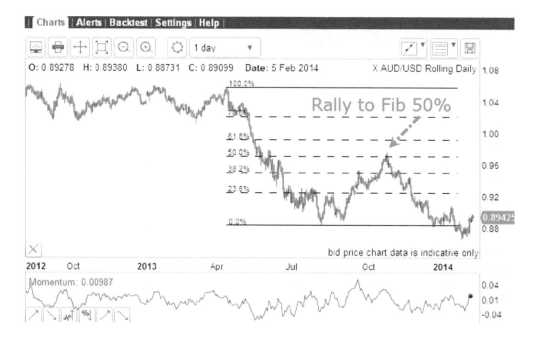

The market made a huge slide from April 2013 to the low in August, but then staged a strong rally, which carried to an accurate hit on the Fibonacci 50% retrace. Once that level was reached, the market felt free to resume its downtrend. That was a superb place to enter short trades, or to exit any long trades on the rally. Of course, once I had this information on the daily, I would go to the hourly chart to identify a good entry point.

In all of the above examples, taking a trade at or very near the Fibonacci level enables a low-risk entry because your protective stop can be entered just a little away from the level. And you would be trading with the main trend, which is the preferred stance in most cases.

3.8 Using basic Elliott Wave Theory concepts

A complete study of the Elliott Wave (EW) Theory and its application could take a lifetime. Luckily, with only a knowledge of the most basic of its elements you can be a very competent EW trader in a fraction of this time. And with this knowledge, you can have insights that very few traders possess, giving you that vital edge.

Basically, if you can count to five, you have that edge!

Elliott Wave – the primary concept

The primary concept, which has been demonstrated time after time, is that in a major impulsive bull or bear market, the extent of the move takes place in five clear waves. Three waves (labelled 1, 3 and 5) are in the direction of the main trend and two are counter-trend (labelled 2 and 4). By *impulsive*, I mean the direction of the pattern is the same as the one of the larger-scale trend.

The big take-away is that if you are in a suspected fifth wave, get ready to take profits and prepare for a counter-trend move.

Trading the third and fifth waves

Figure 3.8.1 shows a great example in the weekly USD/JPY.

The market had been in a major bear run for many years and made a major low in late 2011, the market moved up, then back down, and then in late 2012 it entered into a long and strong bull run taking it above the previous high. That enabled me to label the waves 1, 2 and an ongoing wave 3 (clue: it was a strong move). When wave 3 really took off, that was confirmation I had my labels correct.

Then the market entered a deep consolidation period in a complex wave 4 (note the beautiful triangle pattern) before moving up to new highs in the final wave 5. And note the negative momentum divergence between the waves 3 and 5.

One other confirming clue is that waves 2 and 4 (the counter-trend waves) are of roughly equal size and duration. This is important because if, say, wave 4 was small and of only a few days in length, you would very likely not have a wave 4! In other words, the waves must look right and in proportion.

FIGURE 3.8.1

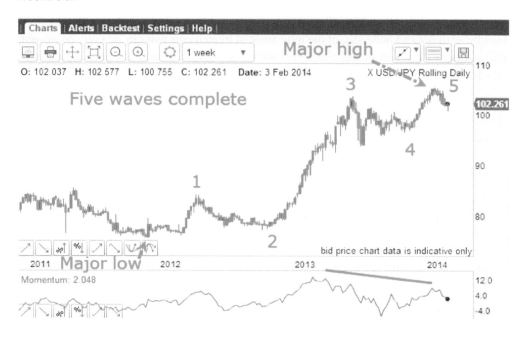

There are several very useful trading tips presented by this chart:

- When the market rallied above my wave 1 high, you could have entered a long trade in the 84 area, suspecting a third wave was in progress. Remember, you could anticipate a huge run when in a third wave, so the rewards for getting it right are immense – so long as you can stay with the trade! That was a great trade entry because you would be trading with the main trend, which is always advisable.

- When the market entered wave 4 and the downtrend line of the very clear triangle was broken to the upside, that was a terrific buy signal (Figure 3.8.2).

- There was a potential profit of over 4 cents available on that trade. The weakening momentum picture in wave 5 gave a clue that the entire bull run was in danger of topping out and a warning to exit the trade soon.

- And because we had a completed five-wave pattern, you could then start to look to trade from the short side, anticipating a new bear trend.

- Many traders would be looking for the market to continue its uptrend at wave 5 because it has been in a bull market for many months and the fundamentals hadn't changed (always a dangerous thought). Remember, markets make opinions. But with your knowledge that *fifth waves are ending waves*, you would have a head-start on most traders if the trend has indeed changed. And it is the selling by the disappointed bulls that will fuel the new bear market. Then, the entire process repeats itself, but in the opposite direction.

FIGURE 3.8.2

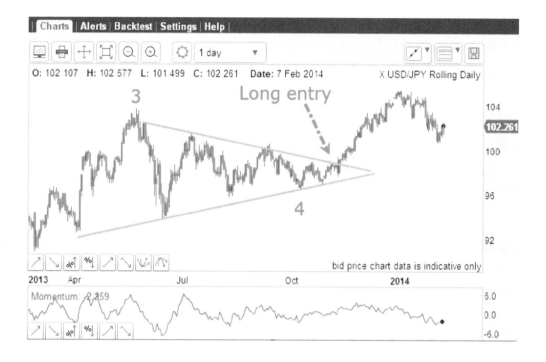

So we had two excellent long-term trades available: the first trading with the third wave and the second trading with the fifth wave – both in the direction of the main trend. The combined potential gain was at least 25 cents, or £25,000 for a £1 bet.

The beauty of this example is that I did not need an intimate knowledge of what Abenomics is and how it works. This is part of a fundamental analysis and occupies many bright minds currently. For me, it is nice to know that it exists, but to make money all I need are the charts and my methods. In fact, the less detail of the fundamentals that I know, the better trader I am.

That is one of the many paradoxes of trading the financial markets – and is why it is in a totally different category from just about any other activity in the real world. Would you put your trust in your brain surgeon if he said that he knew little of the details of his work and all he knew was that lobotomies exist?

Know your A-B-Cs

This is a wonderful pattern that I use time after time, even on the very short-term charts as well as the dailies and weeklies. It enables me to time a low-risk entry to align with the main trend.

Many (but not all) wave 2 and 4 corrections in a major trend occur in three waves, which I call A-B-C. My task is to identify the end of the C wave and then enter the market fading the C wave, jumping on the main trend.

I have several examples of this in the next chapter.

The waves are fractals

You can subdivide any wave and find waves within waves within waves – and they all have a roughly similar appearance. In fact, unless you knew the scale of the chart, it would prove difficult identifying it!

But the main fractal I look for is in third waves of a five-wave impulsive sequence. Within my third wave I should be able to count five clear sub-waves. And within that third sub-wave, I should be able to count five sub-sub-waves, and so on.

In fact, I use this exercise to validate my first third wave count. But I can only do it near the end of the wave. In the meantime, I have to use incomplete information (which is an ongoing limitation for all of us, sadly).

Figure 3.8.3 is an example in the Dow.

FIGURE 3.8.3

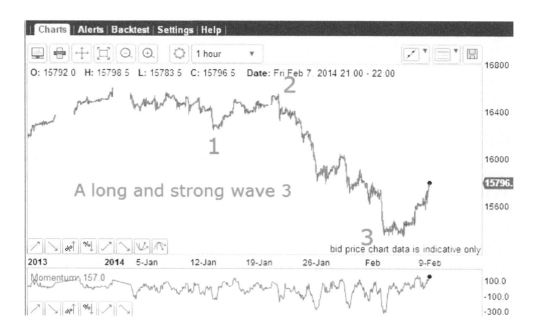

The vigorous decline off my wave 2 high puts it in the third wave category and as the market moved down to the recent low, I was then able to put the wave 3 under a microscope and found what you can see in Figure 3.8.4.

FIGURE 3.8.4

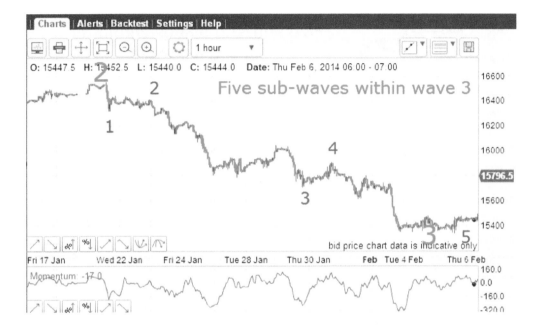

My original wave 3 contains a clear five sub-waves complete with a long and strong sub-wave 3. But that's not all – this third sub-wave contains five sub-sub-waves (see Figure 3.8.5)!

And even more astonishing, this third sub-sub-wave contains its own five-wave pattern.

Markets truly are fractals!

FIGURE 3.8.5

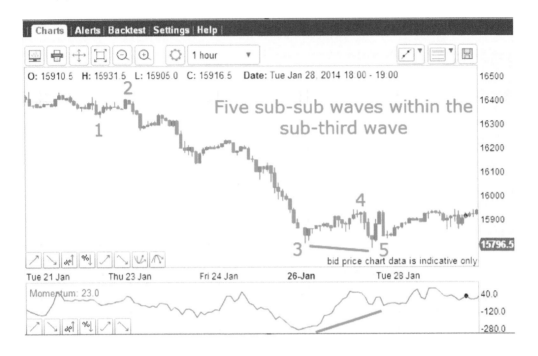

For the all-important trading strategies, having all of these fifth waves ending at the end of my original wave 3 label meant only one thing – the decline was likely over (for now) and a counter-trend rally in a large wave 4 should be expected.

That was the time to cover all shorts and even probe for a long trade.

Can you see that just an understanding of some of the basic tenets of Elliott Wave Theory can give you a tremendous edge? It is a study I heartily recommend.

3.9 Context is key

I am presenting many ideas and concepts that can produce wonderful low-risk trades, but you may be forgiven for believing the various methods can often give conflicting signals. For instance, a tramline break may indicate a short trade, but the market is at the end of a C wave correction, for example, indicating a long trade.

I realise this is a problem and it highlights why we must always weigh the balance of probabilities when trading with any system, including mine. The chart is always tracing out an incomplete pattern. Patterns are only complete in hindsight – when it is too late to profit from it, of course.

We are constantly making projections using incomplete knowledge and that is why trading is part science, part art. And to get a feel for the method much practice is required. But there is no doubt that the act of selecting which signal to use gets easier with practice. When you become familiar with your markets and their personalities, you should get much more expert at trading them.

No one guesses correctly every single time – and that is why protective stops must be used at all times.

I do not recommend you follow more than a handful of the biggest markets, such as the US, UK, Japanese and German stock indices, the major currency crosses such as EUR/USD, GBP/USD, USD/JPY, AUD/USD, and gold, 30-yr Treasury Bonds and perhaps one or two large cap stocks. I would definitely steer you away from the minor currency crosses (unless you have inside information, of course) and most single equities.

When you are presented with conflicting signals, it is always best to go back and review the bigger picture. That should clear up most conflicts.

Figure 3.9.1 is a good example in gold.

FIGURE 3.9.1

The centre line is a long-term trendline from October 2012 and has several accurate touch points before the September 2013 touch point. This makes it a highly significant and reliable tramline.

In the past few days, there has been an upside break of this tramline, which would normally be considered indicative of further gains – perhaps to the upper third tramline target. But the market has been stopped by the resistance offered by the Fibonacci 38% retrace area. This sets up a conflict between the upwards force of the tramline break and the downward force of the Fibonacci retrace.

Is there a trade on? How can I decide?

To determine if there is a sensible trade on, we must weigh up the opposing forces.

In the bullish camp, we have the tramline break and the positive momentum divergence at the low. On the bearish side, we have the established downtrend and the Fibonacci resistance which, if strong enough, will send the market to new lows. Because many traders will be monitoring the long-term tramline, short sellers will have many protective buy-stops above this line at various levels. If the market can get to these, there will likely be a rush of short covering and the market should run up very quickly.

This puts the odds for a rally continuation somewhat higher than the alternative. And if the Fibonacci 38% level can be overcome, the next target is the 50% level. Reaching that level would confirm the tramline break most definitely.

You see, I use lots of "what if" scenarios to make projections and this is the correct mindset for swing trading. This describes the process in a nutshell. And, of course, I always use protective stops in case my guess is wrong.

Figure 3.9.2 is another example in EUR/JPY.

FIGURE 3.9.2

I have an excellent tramline trio full of accurate touch points and the market has recently touched the centre tramline from above. That makes this an opportunity for a long trade, according to the Tramline Trading Rule.

But the big move up is a clear five-wave sequence and the final fifth wave has been put in, which means the main trend is now down.

So there is a clear conflict between the bearish implications of the EW count and the bullish scenario of the tramline support.

In light of this bearish EW picture, is the long trade advisable?

Yes, it is. That is because we are using the Tramline Trading Rule correctly and have a low-risk entry with our protective stop just under the centre line. Also, we don't know for certain that the fifth wave has actually ended yet. It may extend and go on to make new highs before topping out. We must give the long trade the benefit of the doubt.

If we are wrong, the worst case scenario is that our trade is stopped out and we add one more small loss to our loser account. And if this occurs, it means the centre tramline is broken. This would confirm the new downtrend and we can feel free to reverse our position and go short on the break.

Summary

In this chapter I have outlined the various techniques I use for uncovering trade setups and how I enter and exit those trades. Of course, if a pattern is potentially unfolding that you believe you recognise, it may or may not turn out to be that pattern in the fullness of time! We are always dealing with uncertainties. The main concept is that context is key. If you are in a well-defined fifth wave then you should be looking to trade against the former trend and/or take profits on existing positions.

In the next chapter, I reveal my five favourite trade setups, all of which allow for low-risk trades to be made.

CHAPTER 4

MY FIVE BEST TRADE SETUPS

In this chapter I give my Top Five Trade Setups. If you do nothing else but specialise in these, you should have a very successful trading business.

The first four setups take advantage of counter-trend moves to position for the one larger trend. The idea is to identify the maximum extent of the counter-trend waves and then take a low-risk/high-probability position against it and then ride with the main trend, since that is (usually) your friend.

The third wave setup is different. Here I am trading a breakout and as such the risk is higher. But when you catch a good strong one, it is like holding a tiger by its tail; the rewards can be spectacular as you will be riding the new strong trend.

The five setups are:

1. The A-B-C setup

2. The tramline break and kiss

3. The Fibonacci 62% retrace

4. The tramline bounce

5. The third wave

4.1 The A-B-C setup

This is a very powerful yet simple setup that occurs time after time on charts. Not only does it give me highly accurate entries, but it allows for very close stops, thus giving me those high probability/low risk trades I just crave.

Many of them work like clockwork and when you get proficient at spotting them, it makes trading seem so easy (but we know it's not!). After becoming proficient you may be able to anticipate the turn just before it occurs and watch it develop as if you had directed the market yourself. That is a very powerful incentive to learn your A-B-Cs.

When a well-developed trend is in place, we normally get several three-wave counter-trend relief moves along the way. The most common form of this is the A-B-C pattern. The rule I use is this: when I see a clear three-wave A-B-C in a trending market, I have confidence that the trend is intact and I will look for a trade with that trend.

Why is the C wave important?

The C wave is important simply because this wave signals the end of the entire counter-trend move and a trade taken here will get you on board the main trend at low risk. Remember, when we can identify a complete impulsive five-wave move, the ending fifth wave sets up the counter-trend move. When you believe the fifth wave is ending, then you can be prepared for the relief move. And when you spot a genuine three-wave move, it is always running counter to the main trend. Trading with the main trend is always the preferred route and this will be accomplished when fading the C wave. By fading I mean to trade against the direction of the C wave.

A great example in GBP/USD is shown in Figure 4.1.1.

FIGURE 4.1.1

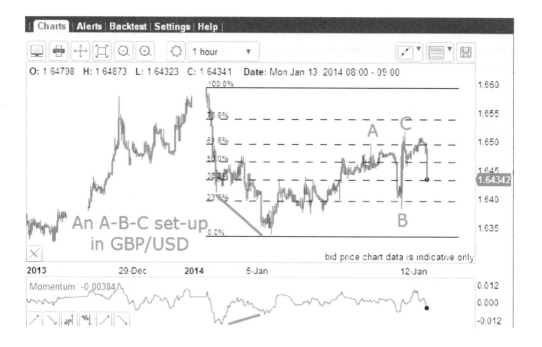

The move off the 1.66 high in early January is in five waves and the fifth wave sports a large positive momentum divergence. That was the clue that the downtrend was about to be interrupted. The market then made a nervous rally off the 1.6340 low until the day of the volatility-inducing monthly US jobs report (the non-farms), where it underwent wild swings, first down and then up. This down-up sequence traced out a nice A-B-C on the hourly chart.

And now we can bring in the Fibonacci levels using the most recent major high and low as pivot points.

Where are the most common turning points for the corrective rally?

> In an A-B-C corrective pattern following an impulsive five-wave move, the most common point where the C wave turns is at the Fibonacci 50% or 62% level.

I sometimes see the 78% levels as turning points, but they are less common (there is one in the next example, though).

Here, the A wave terminated at the 62% level with a fairly accurate hit and the C wave has just exceeded that level. This is important because it illustrates a rule I have observed over the years: when we see a deep A wave to the 62% level, the C wave will usually poke just above that level **and turn at the 67% level**. This is a Fibonacci 2/3 ratio, and lies between the 62% and the 78% levels.

> My advice when using Fibonacci levels is to keep your eye on the 67% level (you will have to work it out manually using your calculator).

A short trade at the 62% level – at 1.6490 – could be protected by a 60 pip stop at 1.6550, which lies just above the Fibonacci 78% level. This would allow for an extension of the C wave to the next Fib level. But now the market has headed down again, this stop can now be moved to the 1.6500 level, which lies at the overnight minor high.

So now I have a trade with a 10 pip risk and a profit target of at least the 6 January 1.6340 low, which is a minimum profit of 150 pips, giving a reward/risk ratio of 15:1. That is one superb setup. Of course, once my target is reached, I will be looking over the market action to set a new target, if appropriate.

The key here is that you must wait for the C wave to be clearly identified. The temptation is to either jump the gun (if you are an impulsive trader), or wait too long after the turn has been made to *make sure* (if you are a cautious trader). You must strike as close as possible to the Fibonacci level to ensure a low-risk trade.

A few hours later and the market has dropped sharply and is within pips of my first target at 1.6350 (see Figure 4.1.2).

FIGURE 4.1.2

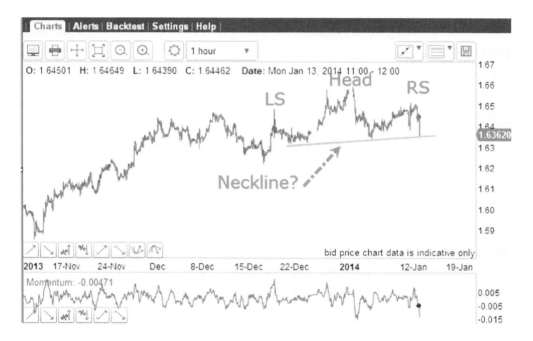

I have expanded the chart so that I can show the big rally in November and December. Now the picture looks decidedly different. I have a potential Head & Shoulders top (see Section 1.3) and the market is currently testing the neckline.

That is a drop of almost 150 pips in two hours and so the question arises: is this part of a third Elliott wave?

Third waves are long and strong and this one qualifies with the momentum reading in the basement. If so, the rally to my RS is wave 2 and we are currently in wave 3, which should take the market well below my neckline.

With this in prospect, I will take partial profits and leave open the remainder, moving my stop on to breakeven point and waiting to see how the market develops. But this has all the signs of a very good downward break up ahead. If not, then my remaining trade will be a wash. I already have some profit in the bank, so no problem.

Figure 4.1.3 shows another great example in the daily chart of EUR/GBP.

From the 1 August high, the market has fallen in a five-wave impulse pattern with the third wave strong and a positive momentum divergence at the fifth wave low. This is pure textbook behaviour, as is the three-wave A-B-C following it. Not only that, but the C wave terminates precisely at the Fibonacci 62% level on a negative momentum divergence (shown with the downward sloping bar on the momentum chart).

FIGURE 4.1.3

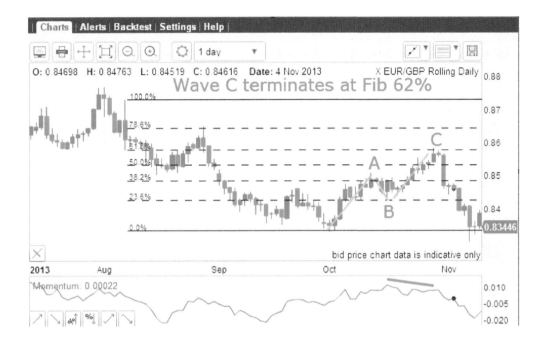

Where is the ideal trade?

This was a terrific setup for a short trade at the C wave high. The protective stop could be placed only 20 to 30 pips away very safely. As the C wave was in progress, all you needed to do was watch the momentum (to ensure it was staying lower than the value at wave A). As the market approached the 62% level you could enter your limit sell order and, when filled, enter your protective stop.

What is my target?

In these setups, my minimum target is always the start of the A-B-C (here at 0.8340). For a short trade entered at 0.8560 (stop at 0.8590), the minimum reward/risk ratio is a very satisfactory 8:1. The target was reached in just over a week for a gain of 220 pips.

So this is the plan:

1. Every day, look for a trending market, then see if there is an A-B-C pattern that is close to completion (in the C wave).

2. Apply your Fibonacci levels and see if the market is getting close to the 62% level (or perhaps the 50% level).

3. Look for budding momentum divergences.

This should give you a great setup to trade with the main trend. You can do this on the daily and hourly charts. Make this a daily routine.

I call this setup a **Five down, three up** for a bear market, and *vice versa* for a bull market.

Figure 4.1.4 shows an example that is a variation on this theme in Eli Lilly (NYSE: LLY).

FIGURE 4.1.4

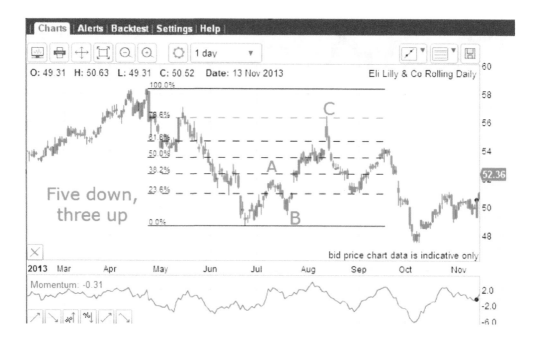

I have a five down off the April high and the customary A-B-C counter-trend rally, only this time, the C wave has carried deeper to the Fibonacci 78% level and with no momentum divergence. This is unusual, but not rare, and you can go ahead and trade it as usual.

But if you had shorted at the 62% level, you would have been stopped out on the continuation of the C wave. When it headed for the 78% level, that was the opportunity to re-enter. Incidentally, the momentum as the market was rallying into the 62% level was already higher than that at the A wave high, so that was a clue that the market likely had further to run in wave C.

When wave C was in, the market declined in three waves down to my target at the start of the A-B-C at the $49 level. That was a great move of $7, or 700 pips in two months.

You can take advantage of further potential gains using the Split Bet Strategy.

Split Bet Strategy

When these setups occur near the start of a new trend, as they tend to do, using the *Split Bet Strategy* pays big dividends. By this I mean you bank a profit on part of your total bet when the target is met (at the start of the A-B-C) and leave the other part open with a protective stop moved to breakeven. This will afford you the opportunity of staying with the trend if it decides to make a really big move in your direction. Then you can calculate a new target.

Imagine your peace of mind when you have a profit in the bank and a trade that, at worst, will break even. The most anxiety-fuelled period for any trader is just after you have placed your trade before either your stop or your target has been hit. This anxiety can only increase if you fail to take profit at your target, or if you take the profit on your full position at the target, and then see the market sail away in your direction without you. Anxiety will be met with frustration – and that is no state for a trader to be in, believe me.

I highly recommend you implement the Split Bet Strategy in all of your trades. Get some profit in the bank and let the market work on your remaining position where you will feel much less tempted to grab a profit on it too soon. This second position may turn out to be a long-term hold and give you a major profit. Some of my long-term whale trades have been made using Split Bets.

Figure 4.1.5 is a great example in BP (NYSE: BP).

FIGURE 4.1.5

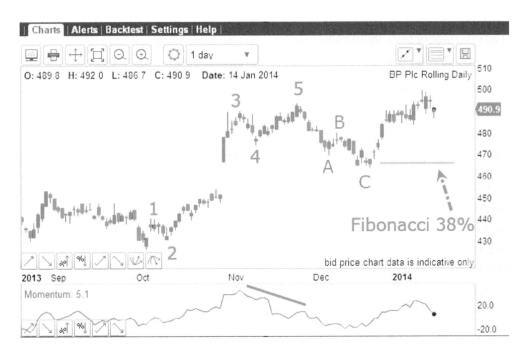

From the 1 October low, I have a clear five waves up with the third wave so strong there is a large gap at the mid-point.

This gap is significant.

Most gaps get filled in due course, but not all do. Those that don't fill very often give a clue that the trend will continue. Look upon an unclosed gap as a sign of strength in the trend. In other words, mind the gap!

After the fifth wave was put in on a very large negative momentum divergence, the market entered a textbook A-B-C corrective phase with the C wave reaching the Fibonacci 38% level. The market then had the option of descending to the usual 50% level, but that would have closed the gap. The vital clue that the gap was repelling the market upwards occurred when the market rallied above the B wave high with force. That was a sign to get long if you had missed the earlier entry.

The market has rallied back to the start of the A-B-C (at the wave 5 high), where a short-term profit can be taken. But this chart is showing the main trend remains up and the most comfortable stance is trading from the long side.

4.2 The tramline break and kiss

Not all tramline breaks are created equal! Remember, the break tells you that the trend has changed and it is better to be trading with this new trend. Some tramline breaks turn out to be head fakes, but when we do get a genuine break, you always have two options for a trade.

The two trade options are to either:

1. set an entry stop order just outside of the line to catch the break, or

2. wait for a kiss back on the line.

Figure 4.2.1 shows a great example in EUR/USD.

I have a superb upper tramline on the daily chart with a PPP two months before the trading channel, making it a very reliable line of resistance from November onwards. Note the most recent assault on this line in late December was repelled vigorously as the market spiked up and then down. My lower tramline has three accurate touch points and when the break occurred it was clean and sharp. That is where a sell-stop order could have been placed.

Let's assume you have entered a short trade on the tramline break. Now the market is trying to get back to kiss the line and is trading above the entry. In these situations, there are three options:

1. The market may fail to kiss the line and resume its descent. That would indicate extreme weakness.

2. The market may go on to kiss the line and then turn back down, where a low-risk short entry could be made (if you had no existing position) – this is the classic *Farewell Kiss*.

3. The market may brush off the kiss and sail on upwards.

FIGURE 4.2.1

The best low-risk option for a trade is the second, where you wait for a kiss on your reliable tramline, set your limit order to short at or near it, and place a close stop just inside the channel in case the market decides it likes option three. In EUR/USD market, you can usually set a 30 to 40 pip stop maximum. And when your target is at least 150 pips away, that gives you an acceptable reward/risk ratio of at least 4:1.

Figure 4.2.2 shows how this developed over the course of the next few days.

The market did come back for a kiss but instead of moving down in a Scalded Cat Bounce, it had another near-miss kiss before moving sharply lower. If you were shorting on the first kiss, you were in danger of being stopped out on the second rally. But that was a second opportunity to position short, since the tramline break was confirming a high probability trend change to down.

FIGURE 4.2.2

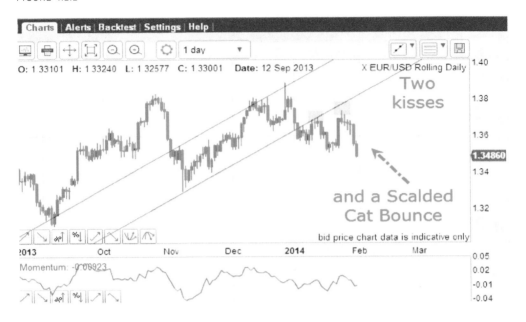

A fascinating and instructive example of this in crude oil is presented in Figure 4.2.3.

FIGURE 4.2.3

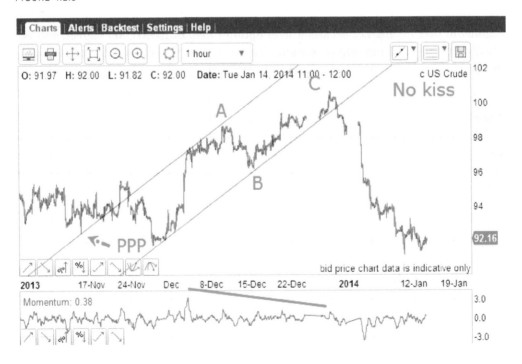

I have a superb lower tramline with at least five touch points and my upper tramline has that lovely PPP and takes in the multiple highs in early December. The tramline break came near the end of December, and what a break! It was so powerful that it couldn't even stop for a goodbye kiss.

Were there other clues that a short trade was well worth pursuing?

We had a few clues that the break would be sharp before the event. First, the final rally topped out a considerable distance away from the upper tramline, which indicated an underlying weakness in the C wave. This indicates that the buying power was not enough to get the market to the upper tramline. This is bearish action.

Second, the entire rally is in three waves and the final wave sported a huge negative momentum divergence, indicating the buying power was being used up in getting to the top.

> Remember, the greater the momentum divergence, the stronger the counter-move.

As the market declined, it was clear that the rally was an A-B-C, so you could set your target at the start of the A-B-C at the 92 area. A short trade on the tramline break would have made a cool 700 pips profit in about two weeks. Nice work. And you could have entered a very close stop for a very high reward/risk ratio trade.

Incidentally, the B wave is also in a clear A-B-C, which is textbook EW. I like to see three sub-waves in the main B wave.

> One other point: in sub-waves, the maximum momentum reading rarely appears at the extreme of the wave.

If you look carefully, you will see the A wave contains a pretty five-wave pattern of sub-waves. The third sub-wave is the very strong thrust moving above the previous highs from November. The highest momentum reading occurs during this third wave and not at the end. That is entirely typical. Look for the maximum momentum readings somewhere inside the third wave, not in fifth (which are generally weaker). Of course, in downtrends, the momentum in third waves will be lower than in the fifth wave.

Figure 4.2.4 shows another example in EUR/JPY.

FIGURE 4.2.4

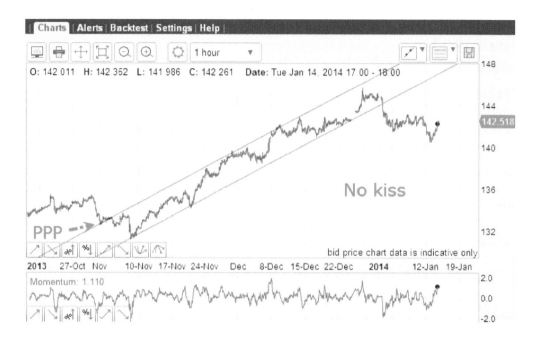

This is a terrific tramline pair with the lower line having five well-spaced touch points and the upper tramline with the excellent PPP and at least four touch points. For two months from early November until early January, the market kept trading strictly within the trading channel. But trading channels do not go on forever and the break occurred. It was a sharp one, which is typical following a lengthy trend.

If you were without a position during the rally, a sensible course was to look for a trend change and to trade the tramline break. This could be achieved by placing a sell stop just under the tramline and adjusting it as the market continued up.

A close-up is shown in Figure 4.2.5.

I have marked where the sell stop can be raised until it is hit. This is a good technique which can be done every couple of hours or so. And the advantage is that you can set your stop before retiring for the night. In the morning, if there has been a big down move, you will have a position at a good entry. How disheartening to switch on your computer and see the market you have been stalking for days on end made a big move in the overnight market without you being on board.

Of course, you can use this technique as a trailing stop method if you are long and wish to protect as much of your profit as you can before the trend change.

The market made a strong move down after entry and a 200 pip profit was available on the first leg down. At no time was the trade in loss.

FIGURE 4.2.5

Yet another terrific example of a tramline break and kiss in USD/JPY is shown in Figure 4.2.6.

The market has broken the lower tramline and has moved back up for a kiss on the underside of the line and is currently backing off. Now I can place the Fibonacci levels on the last wave down and observe that the market has carried to the precise 78% level (see Figure 4.2.7). This is a textbook place to start looking to enter a short trade with a protective stop just above the tramline in the 104.70 area for a 30 to 40 pip risk.

FIGURE 4.2.6

FIGURE 4.2.7

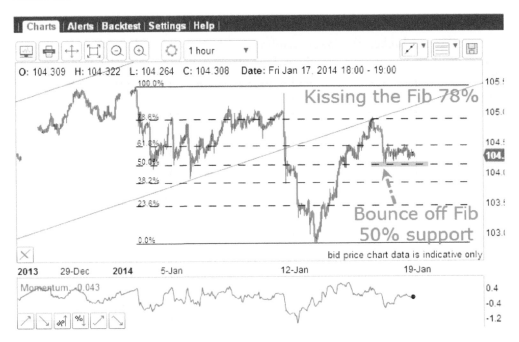

Figure 4.2.7 is a close-up showing not only that the market has kissed the tramline, but also that it has rallied for a highly accurate hit on the Fibonacci 78% level. Remember, when a kiss meets a Fibonacci 50%, 62% or 78% level, that represents extra powerful resistance (or support in the case of a down-sloping tramline).

A short trade here was super-low risk and a protective stop of only 20 to 30 pips could safely be employed.

Figure 4.2.8 shows another good example in AUD/USD.

FIGURE 4.2.8

The market was in a steady downtrend until the upper tramline break on 10 January. This was the first signal that the trend was likely to change. The rally could not hold and the market retreated right back to the upper side of the tramline in a kiss.

This is presenting a low-risk long entry since your protective stop could be placed only 20 to 30 pips away. Figure 4.2.9 shows a close-up of the situation.

Note the market also has retraced 78% of the large wave up from the 0.8850 low. This meeting of the tramline and Fib level represents extra-strong support.

FIGURE 4.2.9

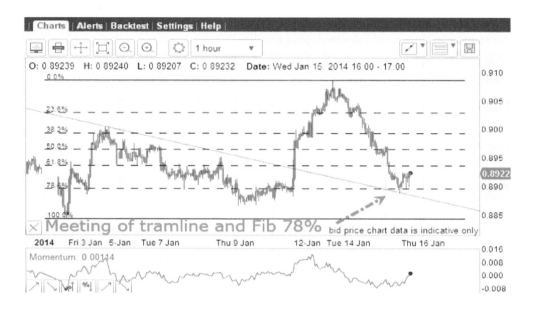

> When you see a meeting of a tramline with a Fibonacci level, this is an area of extra-strong support/resistance.

Making an entry in these areas is a very high probability trade. Make sure you have your Fibs and tramlines working at all times.

Figure 4.2.10 shows a budding example in Apple.

The market has been in a solid uptrend since July with an excellent lower tramline, which has recently been broken. The market has now made a kiss and bounced off it. Momentum is weakening as the rally extends, which adds to the evidence that a major turn is likely.

A short trade on the kiss could be protected by a close stop to give a low-risk trade.

FIGURE 4.2.10

But I have a warning for this setup: if you have a steep tramline pair working and you decide to enter on a tramline break, if the market then reverses and makes a kiss back on the line, the rally to the kiss may be many pips away from the original tramline break and your entry. You may then have to suffer a large adverse move before the kiss is complete and you may be stopped out. You can see what I mean by referring to Figure 4.2.11.

Figure 4.2.11 is the hourly EUR/JPY chart and the tramline break. Shorting on the break at the 143.80 level would make sense, but where to place your protective stop? Because of the steep slope of the tramline, it would have to go inside the trading channel, perhaps to the 145.40 level, giving a risk of 160 pips; which, for swing trading, is far too wide.

You would therefore pass on this trade and hope the market rallies for a kiss to give you a much lower-risk entry. So far, the market shows no inclination of kissing the tramline and you may have missed a trade in this market. OK, so move on!

I have shown many examples of tramline breaks and kisses in this section; that is because they are among my favourite trade setups. In these examples, there are many very sharp moves, allowing for a rapid build-up of profit right from the get-go. I like to see a trade in profit right away and dislike it when the market vacillates around my entry.

I have gained a fair bit of experience of dealing with adverse moves over the years. But for novice traders the stress levels could affect judgment. This is why I recommend searching out these tramline break-and-kiss trades.

FIGURE 4.2.11

4.3 The Fibonacci 62% retrace

We have met the A-B-C setup where very often the C wave terminates at the 62% retrace of the prior five-wave pattern. But we do find situations where there is no clear prior EW pattern and where a counter-trend move makes a Fibonacci retrace of the previous wave down.

Refer to the hourly Microsoft chart in Figure 4.3.1.

From the early December highs the market has dipped down to the 35.50 level and then staged a rally. There is a possible five-wave pattern to this decline but, to me, it is not clear. Also, the rally does not have a definite A-B-C form. I abandon looking for EWs here.

> When looking for the correct EW labels, if it does not stand out right away, then it is probably best to stop looking.

But the rally did carry to the precise Fibonacci 62% level even without being able to identify the EW labels. This was a superb place to short the market. The first target is, as in the case of the A-B-C setup, the start of the relief rally at the 35.50 level, which was duly hit for a potential profit of $2 a share in a little over a week.

This method works particularly well on long-range charts where the EWs are hard, if not impossible, to label.

FIGURE 4.3.1

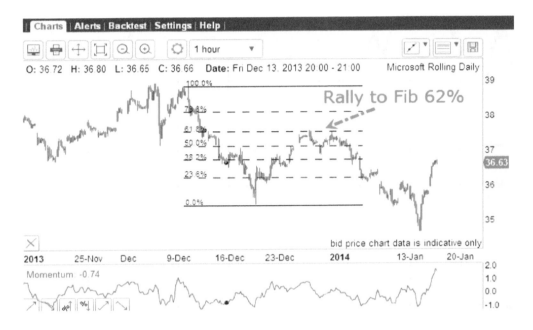

Figure 4.3.2 shows EUR/USD spanning three years.

From the 2011 highs and the 2012 low, the market has rallied to the Fibonacci 62% level twice. The first rally lead to a decent and tradable 500-pip pullback. The latest hit in the 62% level has produced a pigtail spike, which is common after a previous hit has been made on that level.

Why was there a spike high on the second hit?

There are always many protective buy-stops placed just above a major high and the market just loves to go hunting for them! And here they were located just above the first hit on the Fibonacci 62% level. This was an excellent area to begin a short-selling campaign.

FIGURE 4.3.2

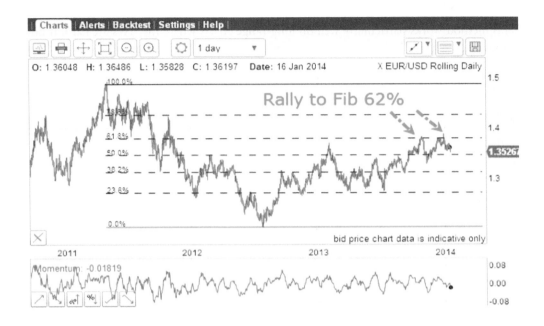

4.4 The tramline bounce

The tramline trading rule states that in a rising market with the tramlines pointing upwards, the correct trade is to go long when the market is trading at or near the lower tramline. The opposite applies to a falling market, of course, with a short trade indicated at the upper tramline. This rule presumes the trend will be maintained and the market will bounce off the support or resistance provided by the tramline.

In Section 4.2, I showed how to handle the situation where the tramline breaks, but here I will explain how I trade with the tramline trading rule.

Figure 4.4.1 is an example in USD/JPY market.

I have a reasonable tramline pair working. There are no Prior Pivot Points, which makes it possible to adjust the slope of the lines without invalidating them as lines of support and resistance.

With this caveat in mind, a short trade here is indicated with the market close to the upper tramline. I am looking for a bounce down off the upper tramline.

But if the market does break above the upper line, that would indicate a likely change in trend and so a close protective stop can be entered. The ideal lower target is on the lower tramline, giving this trade a very high reward/risk ratio, making it a very attractive trade.

FIGURE 4.4.1

Figure 4.4.2 is another example in Alcoa (NYSE:AA), which has been one of my favourite trades since 2013. I previously showed the large wedge that formed on the daily chart in Figure 3.4.1.

Here there is a very good tramline pair with the upper line sporting the two excellent touch points (red arrows). The lower tramline has several accurate touch points with one small overshoot in January.

The correct trade was to go long at the two most recent touch points.

Why go long here and not previously?

The reason is that I could not draw in these tramlines until the most recent touch points were made. But with the added touch points, I now have confidence in these tramlines.

Going long at either of these touch points allows for a protective stop to be entered just below the line for low-risk trades.

And my upper target lies somewhere on the upper tramline, which gives another trade with a high reward/risk ratio.

FIGURE 4.4.2

4.5 The third wave

In Elliott Wave Theory it is usually the third wave of an impulsive five-wave sequence that is the longest and strongest. That makes the task of finding one very worthwhile from a profit perspective. And because third waves are strong, they often do not suffer large setbacks which can take you out of the trade prematurely. One drawback is that your initial risk can be high: much higher than for the other four setups I have discussed in this chapter.

So how do we identify when the market is in a third wave?

To help answer that I need to examine the *context* the market is in. To identify a third wave, I must first locate waves 1 and 2. This is a lot easier said than done in real time.

Let's turn to an example, EUR/USD, in Figure 4.5.1.

The market has been in rally mode and has made a good A-B-C (counter-trend) rally off the 10 November low. If this is correct, then the one larger trend remains down. The A-B-C has given me the context for the next wave and tells me to expect a down move starting from the C wave high.

FIGURE 4.5.1

I have shown my lower long-term tramline and when the market broke below it and through my pink bar, that made the move off the C wave top as possible waves 1 and 2 of a suspected five-wave impulse pattern. And breaking the w1 low gave me confirmation that we are very likely in w3 down following the A-B-C up.

But as with all developing EW patterns, there is an alternative labelling that I need to keep in mind: three waves down so far could be an A-B-C pattern, leading to a renewed rally.

I have my short entry and now I can place my protective stop just above the tramline for a 40 to 50 pip risk.

One of the great attributes of third waves is that once they start, they move rapidly in the direction of the main trend. They are usually very easy to recognise, even when in progress. I now have an expectation for a rapid move lower.

Incidentally, the form of the w1 is also five sub-waves, which gives me the first clue that the downtrend had started off my C wave high.

Summary

In this chapter, I have shown how I trade my five best trade setups and how I manage the trades. The key at all times is to only trade when you can find a low-risk setup and to reject a trade if it cannot offer this, no matter how convinced you are it 'should' be a winner. There are plenty of excellent low-risk opportunities presented in the average week and it is not necessary to take low-quality trades.

Part 3

My Trading Diary

INTRODUCTION TO MY TRADING CAMPAIGNS IN GOLD AND THE DOW

This is my diary of trades and analysis from November 2013 to March 2014 in my gold and Dow campaigns. I chose these two markets because I believed they would offer excellent studies in how I use my methods to extract profits and avoid major losses.

In the Dow, it appeared highly likely that the long bull trend from the lows of March 2009 was ending. Bullish sentiment was off the scale. If I could capture what I thought was to be a major top, then this historic event would serve as the backdrop for some giant moves.

Similarly, in gold, bullish sentiment had reached historic low levels in late 2013 with dire forecasts common. Here too, I believed that a campaign could illustrate how I trade a market from a contrarian perspective.

I wrote my diary in real-time with no after-the-fact editing; I hope it conveys the cross-currents flowing through my mind when in the heat of battle.

THE GOLD CAMPAIGN

Gold was in a major bull market for many years until it made its top in late 2011. Since then, it has been in decline with an accompanying reversal in trader sentiment. From bullishness reaching manic levels near its 2011 high, bullish sentiment reached an unprecedented low – into single-digits – in mid-2013 as measured by the Daily Sentiment Index (DSI). This accompanied the plunge to $1180, which remains the low (so far).

This selling of gold was the flip side of the rush into equities in a low interest-rate (QE/ZIRP) environment.

My campaign is attempting to take advantage of this current bearish sentiment by looking for a relief rally, which could develop into a move of several hundreds of dollars in a huge short squeeze. If stocks do begin their long-anticipated turn down sometime in the next few months, this should propel gold as funds move to its safe haven.

Wednesday 3 December 2013

Gold has been hit very hard in recent months and sentiment is extremely negative. The pundits are falling over themselves projecting lower and lower targets – many below $1,000. This is an ideal setup for a large counter-trend rally.

The big problem is that the main trend is down and it would be very easy to be caught holding a long position when the main trend resumes. That is the danger in trying to trade against the main trend. But when conditions are right, as I believe they are here, a significant relief rally of at least $100 is well worth aiming for.

Figure 5.1.1 displays the monthly chart.

The 2011 top at $1920 was the final fifth wave of the entire multi-year bull market. Since then, the market has declined in three waves, which I have labelled 1, 2, and 3. If we are at the termination of w3, I expect a rally in w4.

The momentum reading is currently very oversold, which tells me the market may be due for a bounce from near current levels.

FIGURE 5.1.1

There is a slight possibility that this entire move is an A-B-C, but this interpretation is less likely. Under either scenario, a rally is likely.

The question is: has the down wave already completed?

I need to look a little closer at the wave structure. If I can spot a complete five waves down within wave 3, I will have a likely termination point.

And here it is, in Figure 5.1.2, satisfying all of Elliott's rules with an especially strong w3 (which itself has five sub-waves). There is also positive momentum divergence building, so I feel I am close to my low.

FIGURE 5.1.2

But I need to see the start of a rally and a push above a minor resistance. Moving on to Figure 5.1.3 we can see the w5 from Figure 5.1.2 on a 15-min chart and I can identify a small-scale, five-wave motive pattern (with long and strong w3). This is really shaping up now.

I decide to place a buy-stop at the $1224 level with a protective stop just under the w5 low at $1210. If the market does decline under my w5 low, I have obviously mislabelled the short-term waves and I want to be out. I will only retain the trade if the market proves my count is right.

My trade is stopped in at $1224 and I enter my stop loss at $1210.

FIGURE 5.1.3

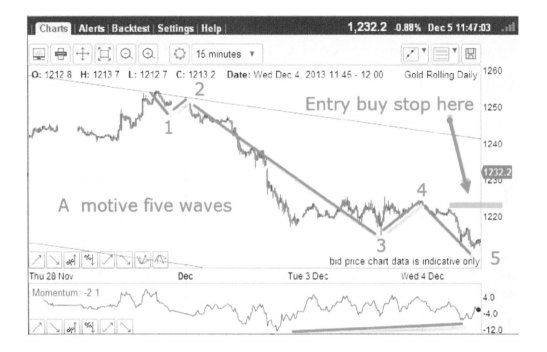

Friday 6 December

Market is rallying nicely; have I found the low at w5?

Today sees the release of the important US jobs picture (Fed taper questions) and sure enough, after the release, the market goes haywire with huge swings down and then a recovery. But crucially, my protective stop has not been hit – my w5 has not been violated (see Figure 5.1.4).

FIGURE 5.1.4

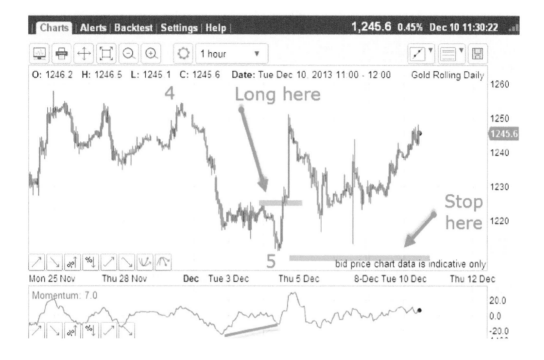

Tuesday 10 December

Yesterday and today the market is edging upwards again and I can now draw new tramlines, as shown in Figure 5.1.5.

I have superb PPPs and touch points going back some way. That is always reassuring when positioning new tramlines. And since 24 November, I have six great touch points on my centre tramline with the market knocking on the door this morning.

If this resistance gives way, we should be off and running to the upside as there is bound to be plenty of buy stops in the zone above the tramline – a swift move up to the upper tramline in the $1270 to $1280 area is on the cards.

But if not, no worries – I have moved my stop to breakeven at $1224 for a no risk trade. Nice.

Now I have a good low, I can apply Fib levels to the wave down off the $1360 high, as shown in Figure 5.1.6.

FIGURE 5.1.5

FIGURE 5.1.6

We can see the rally has carried to the Fibonacci 38% level, where I expect at least a pause (and there is some overhead resistance here from the mid-November trading). So far so good. But I must be aware that the rally is in three waves so far and could be a corrective A-B-C, which would lead to a move to a fresh low.

Thursday 12 December

The rally is not holding and the market has crashed back to underneath my centre tramline. I have been stopped out at my breakeven stop.

- Result: no loss or gain.

Friday 13 December

But I am not giving up on a long trade in gold. My long-term analysis remains valid and I still feel a $100 to $150 rally is likely. If anything, the hedgies are even more bearish (COT shows this).

The market has come back to challenge the 4 December $1211 low, but so far, the low is $1220 – only $10 shy. This sets up the possibility of a new EW labelling, as in Figure 5.1.7.

FIGURE 5.1.7

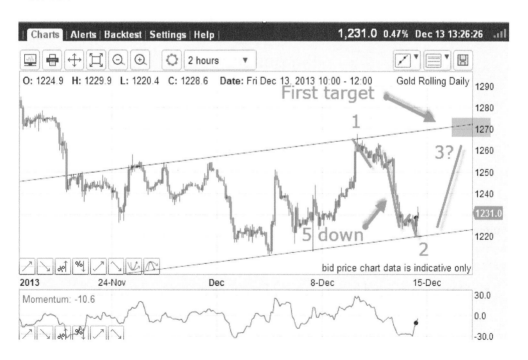

Not only do I have a possible w1, w2 and the start of w3 up, but I have a very tasty tramline pair. The lower tramline takes in the important $1211 low and today's low (w2). It also takes in the precise hit on the spike low on 6 December. That makes three accurate touch points.

Also, I note w2 has five waves, just as the previous w5 had earlier this month.

Could this be the start of the big relief rally?

Figure 5.1.8 shows the developing situation.

FIGURE 5.1.8

The move down off the 10 December high has five clear waves and there is a massive positive momentum divergence at the fifth wave. I set my entry buy stop just above the minor resistance at $1230 and set my protective stop at the 62% retrace of the move up from the $1220 low.

- My trade is stopped in at $1230 and I enter my protective stop at $1224.

Wednesday 18 December

The market has lurched down and has taken me out on my stop.

- I am stopped out at $1224 for a 600 pip loss.

Friday 20 December

I'm afraid it's back to the drawing board for me. Being a persistent one, I am still monitoring gold because with the sentiment at rock-bottom, a low will be made soon – of that I am certain. Now that it is trading under $1200, this is a good place to look.

Why?

Remember the infamous plunge low in late June to $1180? The talk was of manipulation by hedge funds (and central banks) driving all the gold bugs out of the game. And we had a strong rally in July and August out of that low.

The next chart in the sequence is Figure 5.1.9.

FIGURE 5.1.9

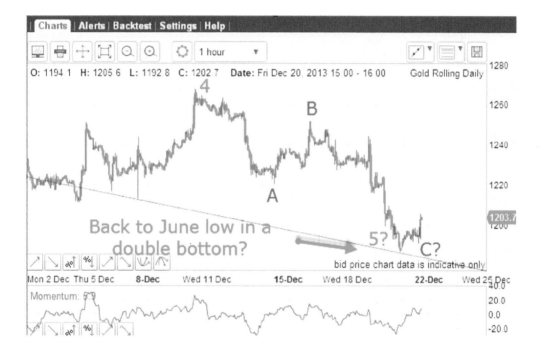

The low yesterday was $1186, so if we can get a rally going from here, that would set up the possibility of a double bottom. That will get the chartists excited!

This is my best guess for the EW labels. Also, I believe I can spot five waves in the C wave. I have also drawn a new lower trendline. It is time to test the waters again with a long trade. You see, I am probing the market for this elusive low because when I get it right, I am expecting the rewards will be spectacular in the short squeeze.

- I have gone long gold at $1197 with a protective stop at $1187.

I have set my stop just under the recent minor lows.

Thursday 26 December

We often see some good volatility over the Christmas and New Year break and this should apply especially to gold. Bullish sentiment at the moment is in the basement (recent DSI at 4% bulls was about as extreme as I have ever seen it).

Now with a new low in place from last week, it is time to redo my EW labels. I note that the low so far is $8 shy of the June $1180 plunge low, so there is a possibility that this could be a rare *truncated fifth wave*. The position with gold priced in dollars and also priced in euros is shown in Figure 5.1.10.

FIGURE 5.1.10

This gives a better fit since the euro price of gold has made a low underneath the June low, thereby making a fifth (and final) wave down. This means the odds increase substantially that we should be at the start of the massive short squeeze. That would set the cat amongst the pigeons and send the hedge funds scampering to cover.

But another possible EW interpretation is shown in Figure 5.1.11.

The summer rally could be wave A of an A-B-C counter-trend rally with the recent dip being wave B and with wave C up to come, which could conceivably carry to the $1500 area – about $300 up from here.

FIGURE 5.1.11

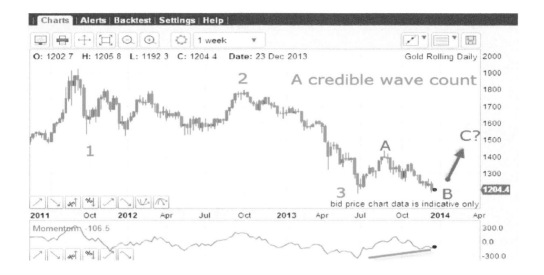

Now do you see why I said this trade has potential and is well worth the effort in catching?

The huge positive momentum divergence really stands out at the B wave low and will allow for a very sharp rally, once it can get started. Whether it is a B wave low or a truncated fifth – either interpretation is consistent with a rally from here or thereabouts.

I have a long trade working at $1197 and now I can move my stop to breakeven. My plan is now to add to longs on setbacks.

The latest COT data backs up my contention that a short squeeze could light a fire under gold. The small speculators added to their short positions last week and now have an almost equal number of short and long futures positions. Remember when they were massively long not so long ago? This is a massive shift in sentiment by the small traders who now show a strong bias to the short side.

Now I can look for new tramlines. See Figure 5.1.12.

My next major resistance is at the Chinese hat. This is where the long-term down-sloping tramline meets the short-term up-sloping tramline. Now if the market can rally swiftly to this area, the move up will look like a third wave off last Monday's w2 $1192 low. But a failure here would likely send it back to test the $1180 low.

FIGURE 5.1.12

Tuesday 31 December

The market is not holding gains and is edging lower.

- My trade is stopped at breakeven at $1197 as the market edges lower.

I am watching as the market is heading down towards the $1180 level (the critical June low) to see if it will suffer more selling and go on to trade well under this level, or to encounter good buying ahead of tomorrow's New Year holiday. I would be surprised if losses were extended much beyond $1180 because of the very crowded short trade.

And I did not have to wait long to find out!

After spending a few moments around $1190, the market took off like a scalded cat. That was my answer. I decided to get long again as it appeared the low was in. See Figure 5.1.13.

So now I was long gold again.

- I am long gold at $1202 with a protective stop at $1188.

If this low holds, I expect a solid rally in the New Year in the short squeeze I have been anticipating. Sometimes, I have to make several attempts at latching on to a trade that I have been researching and consequently take a few small losses or breakevens before getting that solid entry prior to a big move. I believe this one has good potential for that.

FIGURE 5.1.13

Friday 3 January

The rally recovery is continuing with a gap opening just above my short-term tramline (see Figure 5.1.12) and also above my longer-term tramline, which now becomes my centre tramline (see Figure 5.1.14).

OK, I now have much greater confidence that the low of last week at $1182 will hold for as long as a period of weeks and that the trend is now up. My best guess here is that we will see a minor top at any time for the first wave up, then a pullback towards the centre tramline and then a new rally into a new high for the move.

- Meanwhile, I am adjusting my protective stop to breakeven at $1202.

FIGURE 5.1.14

Friday 10 January

The market has edged up all week, except for a nasty spike down mid-week. But the market recovered nicely and is making either an A-B-C up or the start of a five-wave pattern, as can be seen in Figure 5.1.15.

Provided the market can rise above the Fibonacci 38% level, my next target is the 50% level at $1270. But that would set up the possibility we have a third wave up on our hands. Either that, or an A-B-C, which implies an eventual resumption of the downtrend. But so far so good for the continuation of the rally.

FIGURE 5.1.15

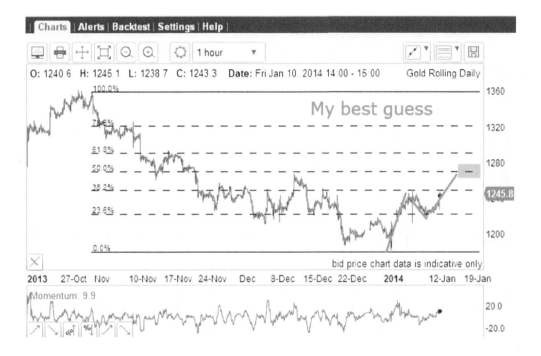

Monday 20 January

The market has been trading according to plan with a gentle bias to the upside. See Figure 5.1.16.

But now the market is testing the upper tramline. It may push through or it may bounce down off the resistance. Discretion being the better part of valour, I decide to take partial profits here on the tramline.

Also, I have been reading more and more bullish commentary lately. Gold did not have a friend as long ago as December! No doubt the gold bugs are looking at gold zooming off into space again after eyeing this $70 move off the $1180 low; they could be raising their hopes once again.

All in all, I decide the best course of action is to take partial profits, since I have over $50 in profits:

- I sell one half of my position at $1256 for a 5400 pip profit

- My net gold position is a profit of 4800 pips and an open trade working from the $1202 level.

FIGURE 5.1.16

I shall continue to hold the other half and move my protective stop up to protect some of the gain to date:

- I will therefore move my protective stop to just under the recent low at $1235.

Friday 24 January

My best guess from 10 January turns out to be correct with this morning's rally to $1270 (see Figure 5.1.17).

My upper tramline has been well broken and the $1270 level is at the Fibonacci 38% level. Stocks have taken a beating in the last week and gold should maintain its rally next week. If not, then something is wrong and I will reassess.

FIGURE 5.1.17

Thursday 30 January

Gold continued its rally towards my second target at the Fibonacci 50% retrace of the wave down off the August $1430 high. See Figure 5.1.18.

This rally has broken my upper tramline but I am suspicious of a big rally here since the entire move off the $1182 low has overlapping waves, which is the sign of a counter-trend move, not the start of an impulsive move up.

I really like my tramlines with the multitude of accurate touch points and, at present, the market is testing the upper line's support.

Will we see a kiss?

FIGURE 5.1.18

Today, the market has fallen hard and I decide to move my protect-profit stop to the recent low at $1235, where I am taken out. See Figure 5.1.19.

FIGURE 5.1.19

- I exit the last part of my trade at \$1245 for a profit of 430 pips.

- My combined profit on the two positions is 970 pips.

I am now flat gold and looking for the next trade.

Monday 3 February

The market has clearly made a tramline break and is now testing support at this line in a possible kiss. This is one of the best low-risk setups (see Section 4.2) and I am willing to re-enter the long side of the market, expecting the kiss to hold. See Figure 5.1.20.

FIGURE 5.1.20

The tramline break could be very significant because if it holds, the odds increase for a big move up – perhaps in my speculative wave C – and a carry towards the A wave high at around the \$1400 area. That would make this a very profitable trade.

- I re-enter a long gold position at \$1245 with a protective stop at \$1235.

Wednesday 12 February

Figure 5.1.21 shows the market edging upwards, but slowly, as it eats into the overhead resistance.

FIGURE 5.1.21

Now the tramline break is looking more genuine, but I will still move my protective stop up to $1250. The market had edged up to a high of $1296 today – only $4 away from the round number $1300. Since this is a Fibonacci 62% retrace of the last major wave down, I decide to take profits on one half of my position.

- I exit one half of my position at $1290 for a gain of $45 and leave the other half position open with my protective stop moved up to $1282.

Monday 24 February

The market continues upwards and has made the Fibonacci 23% retrace of the big wave down off the $1800 high. See Figure 5.1.22.

The test of the Fib 23% level was a clear A-B-C, so the main trend is intact. But now the rally off the C wave low has a lovely little **five-wave continuation pattern**. This is one of the patterns I discussed in Section 1.3.

Now with my wave 5 rising above wave 3, I have confirmation the uptrend is intact.

FIGURE 5.1.22

That means I can reinstate to a full position:

- I go long one half position at $1328 with a protective stop at $1318.

And I will move my protect-profit stop on the other half position to $1305 in any case (just under the 20 February low).

Wednesday 26 February

How does the big picture look now? Let's take a look at Figure 5.1.23.

The market has clearly broken above the centre tramline and heading for the upper tramline, putting my major target in the $1400 region, just where the major high from August 2013 was made.

But the market has zoomed up with no real setbacks since it made the December double bottom, which is why I suspect the move away from the Fibonacci 23% level may not be clear-cut. I believe a decent dip awaits us.

FIGURE 5.1.23

Fib 23% retrace

mid price chart data is indicative only

Friday 28 February

The market has been zigging and zagging over the past two days; the latest DSI sentiment readings are out and it is not a pretty picture for the bulls, as seen in Figure 5.1.24.

The DSI is the daily survey of professional futures advisors in the USA and has reached dangerous levels where major highs have been put in previously. This is a good proxy for the public sentiment on gold.

I decide to move my protect-profit stop on all positions to $1325 and I am then stopped out.

- My profit on one half from $1225 is exactly $100.
- My loss on the recent half from $1328 is -$3.
- My net profit overall is $97.
- Total profit during the campaign is 1940 pips.

The market may rally a little further in the short term, but I will wait for a good-sized dip before looking again at a trade. With sentiment so bullish (and the latest COT confirms this), I believe a $40 to $50 dip should burn off the froth.

FIGURE 5.1.24

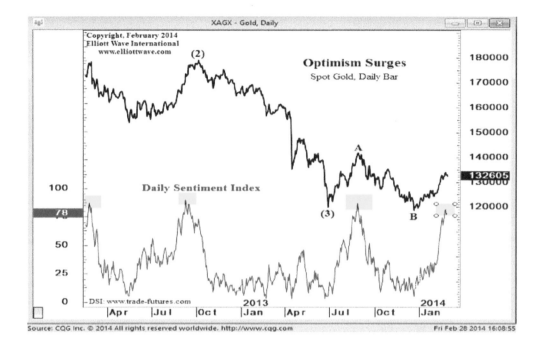

Monday 3 March

There are many bullish noises in the media about increased global tensions (China/Japan and Russia/West) and huge physical demand, such that DSI has climbed even more to the 80 area. This is making me nervous, but I believe there is more upside.

There was a nice strong upside breakout over the weekend and a dip on an A-B-C. The market has corrected 62% of the recent rally and hourly momentum is oversold. See Figure 5.1.25.

There is a large gap created by the strong Sunday night trade and the market is testing it currently. Even if it closes the gap, the odds favour a resumption of the rally. That is why I decide to reinstate my long position here.

- I enter a full long position at \$1335 with a protective stop at \$1325.

I decide on a \$10 stop since even a gap closing would keep me intact and if the market did trade down to \$1325, my rally forecast would not be as secure and I would want to be out of the market in this case.

This trade depends on the C wave holding.

FIGURE 5.1.25

C: 1335.3   Date: Tue Mar 4 2014 14.00 - 15.00   Gold Rolling Daily

Friday 14 March

Ukraine has dominated the news in the last week. I was away on holiday and gold has gained over $50 in this time. I should go away more often! But today I am feeling very nervous. DSI has edged up to a new high at a little over 80% bulls and COT data show specs have filled their boots with long positions.

On the daily chart in Figure 5.1.26, I have my EW labels with the current C wave edging up to test the Fibonacci 78% retrace of the B wave. But I note the looming potential negative momentum divergence as a warning sign.

For this reason, I decide to exit one half of my position at $1385 for a tidy $50 profit in only two weeks for a textbook swing trade.

- I exit one half of my long position at $1385, retaining the other half and moving my protect-profit stop to $1365.
- Profit on this half is $50.

There is no doubt global tensions are ramping up over Ukraine (the referendum for Crimea to secede is held today, Sunday 16 March). The US has promised heavy sanctions on Russian interests, which seem assured. Fear (and madness of politicians) is on the increase, which should benefit gold, but I well remember the armed Russian invasion of Afghanistan in 1980 which marked the top in gold at the $850 area. It was downhill from then on.

FIGURE 5.1.26

Will history repeat?

I decide to play it safe by reducing the size of my longs. When the bulls are falling over themselves to buy, it is usually best to sell it to them!

In the background there is also the China/Japan tension over the disputed islands which has gone quiet of late. Bear markets are marked by increased tensions and a reduction in cooperation between nations.

Monday 17 March

My fears of an over-loved market have proved correct – the market has dropped through my $1365 stop and taken out the last half long position for a very tasty profit (see Figure 5.1.27).

- I exit my final half position at $1365 for a $30 profit.
- Combined profit on both halves is $85.

With today's negative action, it appears my C wave (also wave 4) has ended and I should be looking for a new short trade taking the market down in the fifth wave to below the $1180 lows.

I shall await a rally because the market is testing the Fibonacci 38% retrace now and if the market bounces from here, I will have my wave 1 down in place and will look to short near the top of a wave 2 to come.

FIGURE 5.1.27

Overall, I am happy with trading so far and I am encouraged that I have been able to keep on top of the major swings – thanks to Messrs Elliott and Fibonacci. They really were geniuses and I am most thankful for their work!

Summary

This has been a most successful campaign over fourteen weeks from December 2013 to March 2014. I have made several swing trades in this campaign which resulted in 2790 pips of profit. I have used many of the patterns I describe in the book and have used solid money management rules to protect me against major losses.

THE DOW CAMPAIGN

Before beginning this campaign I had been bearish on stocks for some time. The bulls have been relying on the mountains of central bank stimulus propping up asset markets (which one day will be withdrawn).

The Dow was in a strong bull phase in 2013, gaining almost 30%. I began my campaign in late November by taking a bearish stance.

But doesn't that fly in the face of my recommendation to trade with the main trend?

It does, but I have good reasons for this, as I will show. I have developed a specialty in finding trend changes early and it so happens that in late November 2013, both gold and the Dow were about to change their medium-term trends. That suited me well!

Tuesday 3 December 2013

I have been tracking the Dow for some time, looking for a top. US stocks have been on a tear since the 2009 lows but the rally is getting long in the tooth and the one stark feature is that this is a very crowded trade with bullish sentiment at or near record levels.

And I know that tops are made when bullish sentiment is very high. With a trade this crowded, when the selling starts I have confidence that the falls will be very sharp. So a short position, if entered with good timing, could work out spectacularly. This sounds very attractive!

But the problem I face is in timing my entry.

How can I pinpoint a short trade in the face of a strong bull market?

On Friday 29 November, I note the S&P has made a Fibonacci target at 1815 and appears to have completed a small-scale, five-wave pattern. On the same day the Dow has just broken my lower wedge line (see Figure 5.2.1). That is potentially bearish.

I know that wedges (or ascending triangles) are often found in the final fifth wave position and are often accompanied by a negative momentum divergence and this is precisely what we have here.

I can count five waves up in the Dow from the October 2011 low (see Figure 5.2.1).

FIGURE 5.2.1

Time to get serious as I have a negative momentum divergence staring at me.

Monday 2 December

On Sunday and into today's early trading, the market has attempted a kiss back to the line but the rally appears very weak. This is shown in Figure 5.2.2, along with the five waves up I mentioned.

The move down looks like it could be a w1 down, w2 up. If the market can drop from here it would be in a w3 down and that could be long and strong.

I have a low-risk trade here because my protective stop can be entered just above the line.

- I shorted the Dow at 16,095 with a protective stop at 15,160.

So now I am looking for a sharp move down in a w3.

FIGURE 5.2.2

Wednesday 4 December

And yes, as you can see in Figure 5.2.3, I have a sharp down move as the doctor ordered. So far so good. The market has dropped to the Fibonacci 50% support level, where I expect some kind of bounce. Perhaps my third wave has ended here and a bounce would be w4, leading to a new low in w5. That is my outline scenario.

Now I can move my stop to breakeven, since the gain is about 200 pips and my original stop is only 65 pips, making the gain almost three times the initial risk. I now have a no-loss trade working.

FIGURE 5.2.3

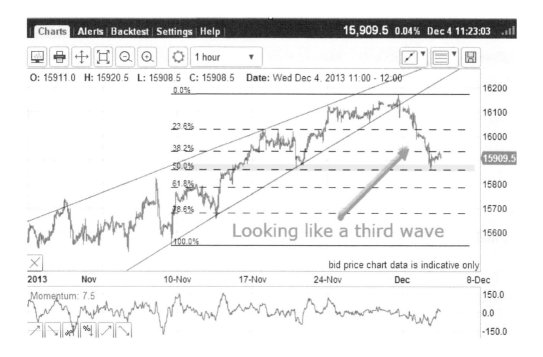

Thursday 4 December

I now have what I was looking for – a five down, just completed – as shown in Figure 5.2.4.

On the 15-min chart I have my five down and it obeys all EW rules as a motive wave (a small-scale five waver that is in the same direction as the one larger trend):

- w3 is long and strong and has five sub-waves within it.

- w3 is not the shortest wave.

- w4 does not overlap the price area of w1.

In addition:

- There is a positive momentum divergence at the w5 low (which shows up beautifully on the hourly, as I switch back and forth between the two charts).

Thus, a relief rally is odds-on. So far it has carried to my upper tramline in one leg up. I would prefer to see an A-B-C rally and this may be the A wave, leading to a B wave down and then a new recovery high in a C wave.

FIGURE 5.2.4

But if this is a very powerful w3, it could extend further to the downside. Also, I do not have total confidence in my tramlines as they have so few touch points, but until I can see a better set I will stick with these.

However, the complete five waves down plus the start of a relief rally means I shall take profits here and look to get back on board at a higher spot.

- I took profit on my short at 15,940 for a gain of 155 pips.

Tuesday 10 December

As I forecast, the market has staged a rally off my w5 low in spite of a negative US jobs report. I guess bad news is still good for the market. What perversity! Still, so long as the market believes what the Fed will do to tapering is paramount, I must go along with that paradigm. But one day the whole house of cards will come crashing down and then bad news will be really bad.

Today, bad news is still good, but for how much longer?

I am looking for an A-B-C off the five down with the C wave ending at a Fibonacci 50% or 62% retrace of the five down. That is the most likely scenario.

I also plot the S&P (see Figure 5.2.5) because it can give a cleaner-looking EW chart.

FIGURE 5.2.5

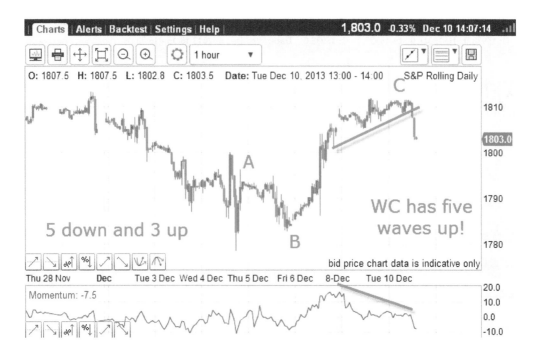

I had a Fibonacci target on the S&P at 1815, which was hit on 30 November; after that the market made a five down and three up (in an A-B-C). The rally has stopped short of the 1815 level and with the negative momentum divergence (and five waves up in WC). This is my moment:

- I entered a short trade in the Dow at 16,030 with a protective stop at 16,060.

I entered my stop just above the high of the rally in the Dow. That gives me an ultra low-risk trade, risking only 30 pips. That is a gift! To be able to trade the Dow and enter a stop only 30 pips away and have an excellent chance of staying in the trade is very rare, to say the least.

Friday 13 December

The market has tumbled and I caught the C wave top. The Dow as it stands is shown in Figure 5.2.6.

FIGURE 5.2.6

- With a gain of 250 pips or so, I have moved my stop to breakeven.

Now I want to see a new low in the trading from Monday to Wednesday next week because the will-they-won't-they-taper Fed minutes to be released next Wednesday should shake up the markets. If I see that, I will take profits on my new short trade and look for a sharp rally to position short again.

The market does expect some degree of tightening from the Fed, which could come in several forms, not just reducing their bond purchases. We shall see.

Monday 16 December

Yes, I have my new low early this morning to make the w5 to complete the wave down. See Figure 5.2.7.

The five-down wave is marked on the chart. It is a classic with w3 long and strong and a positive momentum divergence at the w5 low.

FIGURE 5.2.7

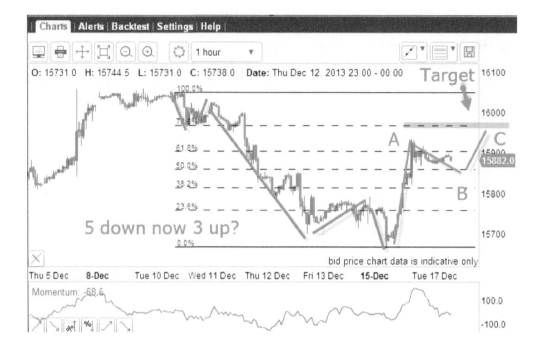

Time to take a profit before the rally gets going.

- I took profit on my short at 15,730 for a gain of 300 pips.

That makes a combined profit on the two trades of 455 pips, which was made on short trading into a bull market. Many would consider that a dangerous game to play, but with low risk entries, my maximum loss would have been manageable even if the trades had not worked out.

Now I am flat the Dow, but still monitoring it closely, as I suspect a major top is close by.

Thursday 19 December

The Fed has spoken! The eagerly-awaited announcement of their intentions with QE is now public – and the US stock markets have taken off like a rocket. I am so glad I took profits on my shorts when offered.

Back to the daily (shown in Figure 5.2.8) and the recent decline is a clear A-B-C – meaning a new high lies ahead.

FIGURE 5.2.8

My top could come at any time now I have a new high print. And the momentum could trace out a negative momentum divergence at any time. We are in a large w5 up (from the June 2012 low starting from the w4 low this October). I am looking for this w5 to top.

Thursday 2 January

Since I expected (and got) a Santa Rally, I decided to sit it out, unsure as I was how high the bullish mania would carry the market. As it happened, the manic enthusiasm to own shares going into 2014 swept the Dow to close 2013 at the all-time high nosebleed level of 16,600! This placed the Dow smack on my upper tramline, as shown in Figure 5.2.9.

I have great confidence in my tramlines; the upper one has a great PPP and catches all of the major tops since early 2012. It would take a massive buying effort to push through my upper line and if the buying is exhausted here it will not take much to see heavy selling drop it back to the lower line again.

It is time to start looking for a top – and a short trade. Today being the day after New Year's Day, the Dow is not yet open but already the German and French indices are trading with large losses following the weak manufacturing data out of the euro zone and China over the holidays.

FIGURE 5.2.9

Actually, I often find that dramatic trend-changing news emerges during long market holidays, such as this one. And with complacency against hazards at record lows (the VIX is back to the 12 to 13 zone again), we have the ingredients for the start of a massive decline starting today.

The chart in Figure 5.2.10 shows a nice short-term tramline pair; the lower line has been broken this morning on the opening.

This is my first signal the top is likely in. My plan is then to wait for a small rally and then take a short trade using the high as the guide for my protective stop.

FIGURE 5.2.10

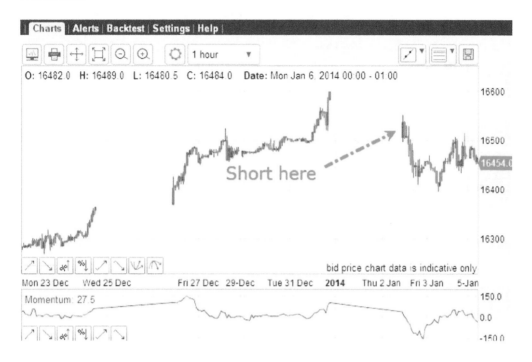

It now appears the top is in, so a slight change of plan:

- I shorted Dow at 16,520 with a protective stop at 16.620.

Friday 10 January

This week the market has been in consolidation mode but today being the non-farms payroll day I expect some fireworks.

And I am not disappointed, with stocks being hit hard. See Figure 5.2.11.

FIGURE 5.2.11

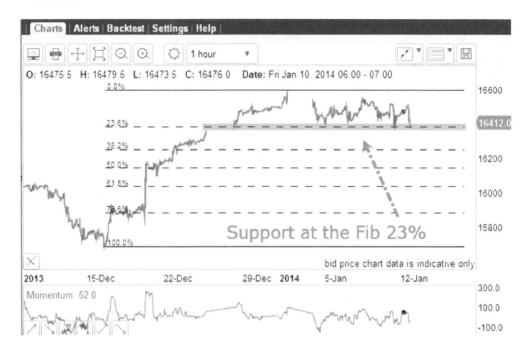

The Fibonacci 23% retrace has been solid support all this week but is being tested again today. When it gives way that will be my signal we are in a third wave down. My first major target is the Fibonacci 50% level at around 16,150.

Tuesday 14 January

The market has broken support and has retreated to the Fibonacci 38% level. See Figure 5.2.12.

This is a good time to review the EWs. I have a five up, that is clear, but this could always be part of a larger pattern. The move down is only in three waves so far and this could be an A-B-C, leading to higher prices. I must keep in mind that although I have found a fifth wave up, that may not be the absolute top.

FIGURE 5.2.12

In light of my uncertainty, I decide to take profits here and sit back and observe. If the market does break down here, I can always find another good entry.

- I take profits on my short Dow at 16,305 for a 215 pip gain.

Thursday 16 January

The market has rallied, as I suspected, but has hit a very interesting point. See Figure 5.2.13.

I have a terrific tramline pair working here. I have the upper line with the rally to it and my lower line takes in the significant gap that was created late in December. Gaps occur very infrequently and when they do it is usually on Mondays after the weekend break, as here. During the week, the markets are open virtually 24-hours.

If this is a *breakaway gap* the move down should be very large and I do not want to miss it. That is why I am probing for a good entry and willing to take a few small losses before latching on to a trade that could net me a very large reward.

Also, I can count a minor five-wave move up from the lower tramline to the upper one. The rally should be done.

FIGURE 5.2.13

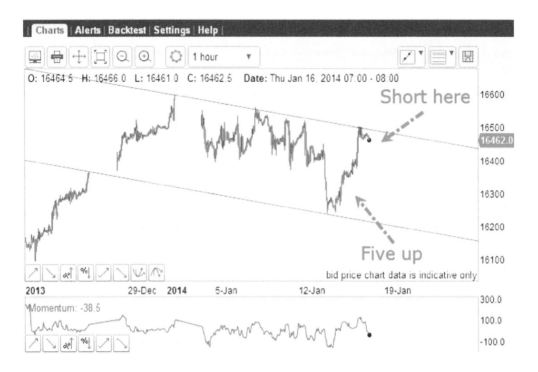

Now, this is an excellent place to re-enter a short trade, so:

- I am again short Dow at 16,480 with a protective stop at 16,520 for a 40 pip risk.

Friday 24 January

The resistance of my upper tramline holds. And what a fabulous move down off it! This has all the hallmarks of a third wave. The chart as I write is shown in Figure 5.2.14.

Now the gap created on the first trading day of 2014 is very relevant. It has not been filled, despite three attempts, making it a breakaway gap. This is a signal that the market wants to follow the gap down very quickly. It signifies a change of trend from the five-year bull market. I am taking it as my signpost for the start of a great bear trend which should last many months.

We are in a clear third wave down now and I am short from near the wave 2 high. I am happy with this position. My policy now will be to add to positions on rallies. In the meantime, I expect the Fib 62% level to be support, at least temporarily.

FIGURE 5.2.14

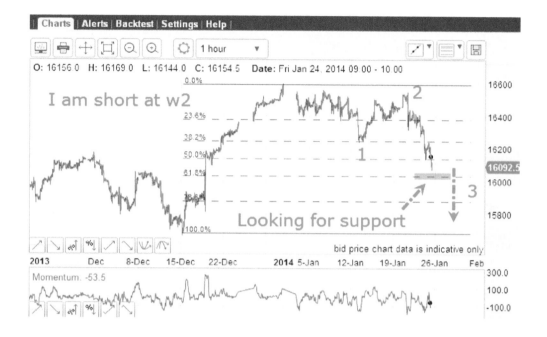

Monday 27 January

We are definitely in a third wave down – the market touched the 15,850 level overnight and is short-term oversold and it appears we should see a wave 4 bounce soon.

- I take profit on half of my position at 15,890 for a 590 pip profit and move my protective stop on the open half to breakeven.

Friday 31 January

Market is testing support at the 15,650 level, as shown in Figure 5.2.15.

This should be very stiff support and since there is a complete five waves down on the hourly chart, odds are good that a decent bounce is up ahead.

And this just in – the AAII investor sentiment report (see the Resources section for more information) shows more bears than bulls. This is a complete switch from the uber-bullish stance in December. The last time bears outnumbered bulls was in August 2012 when the Dow had made a steep decline, just as it has in January. Some things never change!

FIGURE 5.2.15

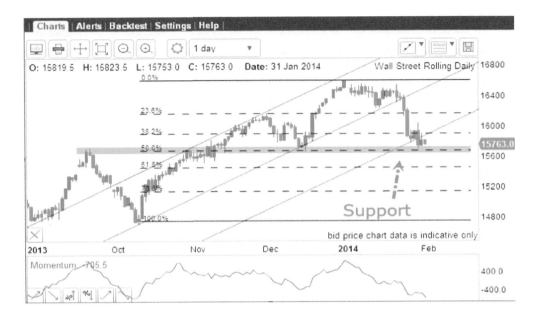

That makes me happy with taking part-profit and holding the other half. My plan is to reinstate the half position when I sense the rally is running out of steam.

Wednesday 5 February

The collapse is relentless – it has moved down and has broken the big support zone. Today I can see a complete five waves down and a positive momentum divergence, as shown in Figure 5.2.16. It is time to tighten my protect-profit stop to 15,420.

That was a great trade:

- I covered my short from 16,480 at 15,420 for a 1,060 pip gain.
- Cumulative profit from the campaign is 2320 pips with no losing trades.

Now it is time to look to go long as I expect a big relief rally up ahead following a complete five waves down (it looks better in the Nasdaq hourly chart). I therefore employ a stop-and-reverse strategy here:

- I reverse positions and go long the Dow at 15,420 with a stop just below low at 15,340 for an 80 pip risk.

This morning, the market has moved up to test the upper tramline. Breaking above that would be interesting!

FIGURE 5.2.16

Monday 10 February

Just when the AAII sentiment survey of US retail investors has registered its lowest bullish reading for many months, the market has staged a vigorous rally (as I suspected), and has hit the Fibonacci 38% retrace in Sunday trading. You can see this in Figure 5.2.17.

The rally has been virtually straight up and my best guess is that this is wave A of an A-B-C. The next move should be down in wave B before a rally in wave C.

I decide to take the profit on one half of my long trade:

- I exit one half of the long trade from 15,420 at the 15,760 level for a 340 pip gain. I am leaving the other half to run with a protective stop at breakeven.

I am using my Split Bet Strategy (see Section 4.1) here and even if the market decides to extend the rally, I am still long on one half of my position. I feel very comfortable with that.

FIGURE 5.2.17

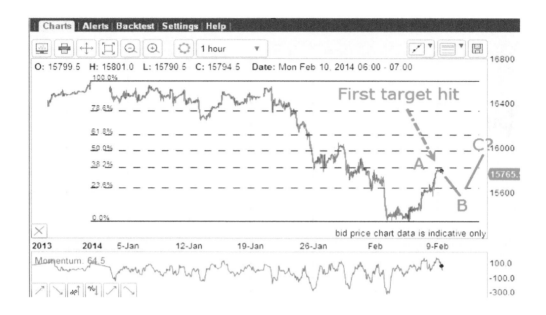

Wednesday 12 February

Rather surprisingly, the market has rallied strongly up and away from the Fibonacci 38% level and reached the 50% level – and has even exceeded it. The rally has been virtually straight up with no obvious A-B-C pattern, as you can see in Figure 5.2.18.

Can it be that this is the A wave high?

I have seen deep upward retracements many times before, so this is not too unusual. My problem is where to take profits on my long position – a nice problem to have.

We are still in wave 4 up, but where will it end?

I am pushing my luck here for further gains. After all, it has been straight up to the Fibonacci 50% level, so I decide to exit the other half of my long trade.

- I exit the last half of my long trade at 15,955 for a profit of 535 pips.

- Cumulative profit on all Dow trades is 3195 pips with no losing trades.

FIGURE 5.2.18

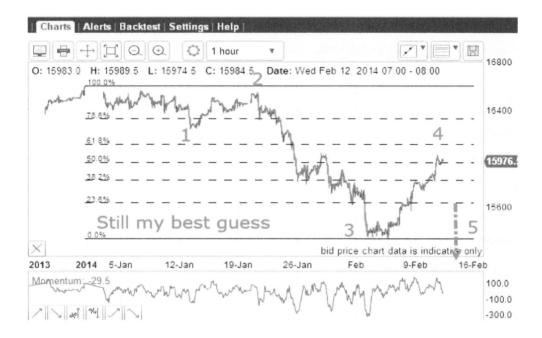

I am now flat and looking for the market to turn around here. And gazing at the hourly chart of the rally, as shown in Figure 5.2.19, I believe I can see five complete waves.

My lower tramline sports at least six touch points (excellent) and a break here should mean the A wave top is in and the market should be heading down in a B wave. If the tramline holds, the market will rally further up to the 62% level. But the negative momentum divergence at the top looks ominous.

I decide to probe the downside and enter a sell-stop order to catch a potential tramline break:

- I enter sell-stop at the 15,925 level with a protective stop at 15,990 if I am filled.

FIGURE 5.2.19

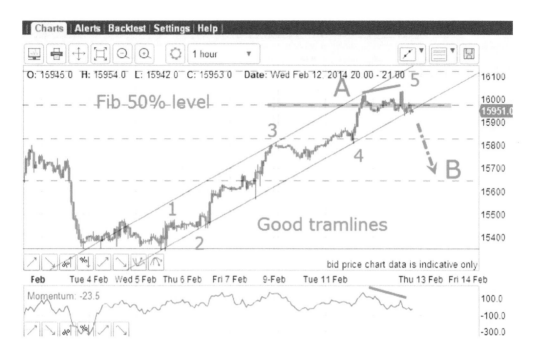

That will position me short once again – a stance I am much more comfortable with. I am not totally at ease trading from the long side because this is a crowded trade and I have learned never to overstay my welcome in this kind of situation.

The market moves down after I am stopped in at 15,925 and reaches a low of 15,850 – a gain of 75 pips. So far, so good.

Is this the start of the big bear market I have been expecting for a long time?

This market has surprised me time after time with its deep upward retracements and I am doing the prudent thing of moving my stops to breakeven.

Later today, the market reverses and I am taken out at breakeven. See Figure 5.2.20.

So that was a wash trade and I have decided to sit this out until I get a better signal.

FIGURE 5.2.20

Friday 28 February

The rally has been relentless and today, following Janet Yellen's testimony, it moved up strongly and then the bottom dropped out, falling nearly 200 pips in less than two hours before recovering into the close.

Now I have a very nice wedge (Figure 5.2.21), which was the pattern I identified at the start of my campaign (see Figures 1.2.1 and 1.2.2).

I like wedges!

My wedge lines possess many accurate touch points. Also I have a pair of negative momentum divergences, pointing to a weakening of the rally force.

The standout feature though is the overshoot yesterday (marked with "!"). Overshoots are usually a clear sign that the buying power is exhausted and the next big move is down.

If the market can retreat to the zone I have marked "Danger for the bulls", breaking the lower wedge line, then the rally should be over.

FIGURE 5.2.21

Interestingly, I have noted a curious symmetry on the daily chart (Figure 5.2.22). The Credit Crunch low was made on 6 March 2009 and next Thursday will be the fifth anniversary of that event. The curious thing is that the single major low along the way occurred around the time when this period is bisected. It took 30 months to reach my B wave low and we are now 30 months this side of that low.

FIGURE 5.2.22

This means that if this cycle is valid, a top is at hand.

Sadly, I shall be away next week and will have the pleasure of discovering whether my theory is correct on my return.

Friday 14 March

Yes indeed, while I was away the market made its top on Friday 7 March at 16,614 and now is trading over 400 points lower.

I feel like the soothsayer to Julius Caesar in 44BC, who warned him to beware the Ides of March (15 March). Caesar was assassinated on that very date, thus fulfilling the prediction. Has the market likewise been topped?

However, my accurate soothsaying has done me no good whatsoever since I was away from my trading desk with no position. But trading is a long-term business and I am confident the market will present me with more excellent entries. It is curious that this top occurred exactly five years and one day from the 6 March 2009 plunge low. This is significant. It points to the idea that cycles, which have fallen off the radar, are back.

All sentiment indicators I have seen are flashing **bear market ahead**.

Over the weekend I read MSM pundits saying there is nothing to get worried about – the bull market is intact and just hold tight. We read the same opinions at every top. But gradually, as the markets work lower, some of them become converted bears, but most do not. The bulls have been right for five years and they are not going to change their tune easily. It will take several thousand points knocked off the Dow to cause them to question their stance.

One data point caught my eye while I was away. China's exports in February were down 18%, while economists were forecasting an 8% rise. That is a 25% miss for the economists. I wonder how many of these experts will lose their jobs?

Figure 5.2.23 is an update on the previous chart, showing the danger zone I indentified earlier at the 16,200 level having been decisively breached.

FIGURE 5.2.23

And now I have good EW labels on the daily, as shown in Figure 5.2.24.

FIGURE 5.2.24

Crucially, the 7 March high did not exceed the all-time high of 31 December. That makes the February rally a wave 2 and it has completed on a large negative momentum divergence.

We are now in the early stages of a large third wave – these are usually long and strong. Getting on board short here will be like trying to catch a tiger by its tail – but it has to be done, since the rewards will be spectacular. I am looking for a break of the 14,800 lows from last year as a possible target for this w3.

Monday 17 March

There has been a nice rally this morning in the hope that the Ukraine crisis will be over soon – a *buy the rumour, sell the news* event. But in Figure 5.2.25 we can see the Dow has made it to the Fibonacci 50% level and this is a great place to enter a short.

FIGURE 5.2.25

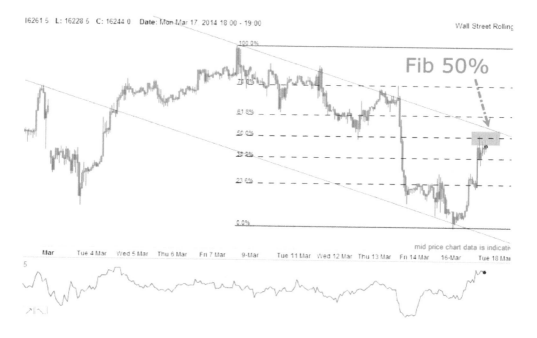

- I short the Dow at 16,255 with a protective stop at 16,330.
- And there we will have to leave it.

Summary

This was also an excellent campaign stretching over 14 weeks. Net profit was 3195 points. As in the gold campaign, I used several trade setups for swing trades as described earlier in the book and employed good money management discipline throughout.

In my campaign I made only one long trade – all the others were shorts. And the main trend was up in a strong bull market – proving that you *can* make money trading against the main trend. I had an overall bearish outlook for stocks and the Dow advanced by 260 pips from my start date of 29 November to the cut-off on 17 March.

So even if I had bought-and-held from the start, I would have made only 260 pips – a far cry from my 3195 pip gain.

I hope this little campaign convinces you that trading the swings is worthwhile.

My Eleven Commandments

I hope I have shown in my book how anyone, whether new to trading or experienced, can quickly gain an expertise that very few traders possess. My simple, visual, chart-based methods can alert you to potentially profitable trades in seconds. But it is one thing to have a great trading system and another to be able to implement it with discipline.

I have seen so many traders blow themselves up by making elementary errors that I offer these, my trading guidelines, which I hope you will find useful.

1. Preserve your capital

There is no dishonour in being wrong on a trade. Take only small losses on your losers and be glad (yes!) because they are small. The winners will take care of themselves. And never, never ever trade without protective stops – they keep you honest. If stopped out, keep analysing the chart for another possible entry.

2. Trade small size most of the time

Keep lots of powder dry at all times for those great setups that do occasionally come along. Keep building your account step by step. Do not look for home runs on every trade – they come along only rarely. They will not make you as a trader. It is the quiet accumulation of modest profits on your winners that will do that. That is how most professionals operate. And do not follow too many markets at the same time. I tend to actively follow three currencies, three stock indices, gold and T-Bonds.

3. Do not get too emotional when you have a big win

If you feel overly euphoric, then it is time to either cut back or stop trading for a few days. Euphoria can seduce you into being bold and making silly mistakes such as overtrading, or trading a market you have little or no experience in and do not really understand but fancy having a go at. This almost always leads to losses. High emotion is good in watching sport or a movie, but it is a disaster zone in trading. Control yourself.

4. Trading is a game where you are trying to find the path of least resistance for the market and flow with that path

Your attitude needs to be one of an interested observer, not a committed opinionated partisan with either a long or a short bias. The market is not the marrying type and you should never be wedded till death do you part to your position – unless it is making money for you, of course. But even then, you will need to know when to demand a divorce.

5. If you have a short run of losers, feel free to stand aside for a few days and compose yourself

If you have been using strict money management rules, you will have most of your capital intact ready to fight another day. But if you have let your discipline slip and have taken a beating on just one bad trade, it will be hard to get back to evens, let alone into profit. Do not let that happen to you, as it does to so many traders. Remember: just one big loss can devastate your account.

6. The methods I present here are simple – and I have deliberately designed it that way

I subscribe to the command: Keep It Simple, Stupid (KISS). Much of the difficulties traders experience come from making their system far too complicated. It is tempting to believe that there is an indicator out there – somewhere – that holds the key to fabulous riches if only you can locate it. These traders spend years and fortunes getting hold of one system after another. These are the Holy Grail traders. Incidentally, has anyone found it yet? All systems are imperfect, but most of the imperfection is within the trader, not the system.

7. If long, become more bearish as the market rises

Also, when you have an excellent profit on a trade, the correct attitude is to become more sceptical of further gains. Most traders do the opposite and become more euphoric and push their targets further and further in their direction. You must learn to control this basic emotion and override it. You need to be taking profits when the *other* traders are euphoric. Do not fall into the trap of seeing a great profit vanish as the market moves against you, as it will. If long, become more bearish as the market rallies and always look for good reason to exit just when the majority are chasing the market up.

Targets should not be set in stone forever. They are guidelines that help plan your eventual exit and can be adjusted in the light of future market action. Sometimes, you will be moving your targets in your direction as more information accrues. You will rarely need to move your targets closer if you have performed a good analysis.

8. It is a proven scientific fact that staring at your screen all day cannot change the market

Sadly, we are unable to will the market our way no matter how long we stare. I have found that the less time I watch the market after I have done my analysis, the better I trade. You may have a similar result.

9. Never trade to get even – that is emotional trading and almost always ends in tears

Only enter a trade after you have performed your analysis using your methods. Do not just jump in on a hunch, either. If you have taken a loss as the market went in the *wrong* direction, keep watching it for a time afterwards, as it may give you another entry signal. Treat this signal as you would any other, erasing the memory of the previous loss. The market doesn't care whether you made a profit or a loss on any trade. And it will always be there for you, so don't rush it.

10. Patience is truly a virtue in trading

Wait for that ideal moment when the trade setup makes sense. Try not to jump the gun in your eagerness to put on a trade. And if you miss a great move, you miss it. Do not kick yourself for missing these, as there will be plenty more coming along the pike. However, when the market hits your target, do not hesitate to take your profit promptly. Do not *see if there is more* after the target has been hit. That way lies indecision and indiscipline, which is quickly followed by ruin.

11. And lastly, trade as if your next trade is likely to be a loser

I know that sounds crazy because we are all encouraged in our real lives to think positive and the good results will follow. It is exactly the opposite in trading! Yes, do your analysis and make your trade based on the objective outcome, but when you believe it may become a loser, you will take very seriously the business of placing an appropriate stop to limit your risk. If you believe your next three trades are likely to be losers, that will concentrate your mind even more on risk management!

Finally, I want to wish you all the luck in the world in your trading career.

To every thing there is a season, and a time to every purpose under the heaven:
A time to be long, and a time to be short; a time to stand aside, and a time to
aggressively trade.

Apologies to Ecclesiastes

Resources

I include here a few resources that I hope you will find useful.

Tramlines

This method is of my own devising. I have been writing as *MoneyWeek Trader* for a few years and have produced several video tutorials on my tramline method, as well as on the Elliott Wave Theory and Fibonacci levels. These are aimed at the novice to intermediate trader and cover the basics.

In collaboration with *MoneyWeek*, I am also preparing a major online trading course for relative beginners which is scheduled to launch in 2014.

www.moneyweek.com

Elliott Waves

The granddaddy and still the most complete source of Elliott Wave analysis and teaching is Robert Prechter's **Elliott Wave International.** I have been following Robert's work for a few decades and his organisation offers a complete range of excellent services, from EW analysis of current markets to a full array of learning resources. I cannot praise Robert's own creative and deeply researched work highly enough.

I recommend for the serious Elliott Wave student his books:

Elliott Wave Principle, by Frost and Prechter (New Classics Library). This is the classic text on Elliott Wave Theory.

The Wave Principle of Human Social Behavior, by Robert Prechter (New Classics Library).

www.elliottwave.com

Fibonacci levels

The Elliott Wave International group offers a good coverage of how Fibonacci levels operate.

General trading ideas

What I Learned Losing a Million Dollars by Jim Paul and Brendan Moynihan (Infrared Press) is a little off-the-wall, but it contains many great cautionary tales. This man lost a million dollars and went through all of the emotional turmoil that losing often produces. His big mistake was to believe and tenaciously hold on to a story, such as: "gold *has* to go up – the dollar is doomed."

I have been following the career of Alexander Elder for decades and was an early purchaser of his first book – *Trading for a Living* (John Wiley & Sons) – in 1993. It contains some excellent insights into the psychology of trading. Elder was an early introducer of the MACD indicator. I can also recommend his other books, including Come into my Trading Room (John Wiley & Sons).

Naturally, almost everyone recommends the classic *Reminiscences of a Stock Market Operator* by Edwin Lefèvre (Traders Press). It is the autobiography of Jesse Livermore, a colourful speculator who was operating in an era when manipulation of markets was relatively easy and commonly done – in the Roaring 1920s when anything went! Has anything really changed in a century? One timeless passage still stands out as great advice today:

> "This describes what I may call my system for placing my bets. It is simple arithmetic to prove that it is a wise thing to have the big bet down only when you win, and when you lose to lose only a small exploratory bet, as it were. If a man trades in this way I have described, he will always be in the profitable position of being able to cash in on the big bet."

Every trader should have a copy of this book on his or her bookshelf – to dip into at frequent intervals.

Current reading

I follow several authors on Seeking Alpha – this is a great way to judge sentiment towards a particular market as a contrary indicator. For instance, if most of the article headings are bullish on a market, a top is probably nearby.

www.seekingalpha.com

I also follow articles in the MSM and find **Ambrose Evans-Pritchard, Liam Halligan** and **Jeremy Warner** in the *Daily Telegraph* to be excellent writers on the economic picture.

Sentiment indicators

I monitor sentiment for signs of extremes and use them as contrary indicators.

AAII Index

This is a weekly survey of retail US stock investors asking if they are bullish/bearish/neutral towards stocks over the next six months.

www.AAII.com

Daily Sentiment Index (DSI)

This site is run by an old futures hand Jake Bernstein and is a daily survey of professional commodity futures advisors (CTAs). The DSI covers a whole range of markets from Lumber to the S&P. This is an often accurate barometer of overall sentiment and I refer to it frequently.

www.trade-futures.com

II Sentiment

Investors Intelligence is also a well-established firm that analyses many independent market newsletter advisories and assesses a bullish or bearish score based on this work. As with all similar sentiment indicators, it is only at extremes of the II Sentiment readings that it becomes useful as a contrary indicator.

www.InvestorsIntelligence.com

Commitments of Traders report (COT)

The US Commodity Futures Trading Commission (CFTC) release data on the long and short holdings of participants in the US futures markets broken down into three categories:

- *non-commercials* (large speculators),
- *non-reportables* (the small speculators), and
- *commercials* (the trade).

It is easy to break down the data into the specs versus the trade.

The COT is released every Friday and is a snapshot as of the previous Tuesday. It covers all of the markets that I trade, except the FTSE 100. At times of extremes, it is a valuable contrary indicator. One of the most useful features is the changes during the previous week.

I trust this data because it is a record of where traders are actually putting their money, which is a much higher level of commitment than answering a survey, where no money is at stake.

Many traders follow the commercials and will look to go long when the commercials hold a large long/short ratio (and *vice versa*). Because the commercials (those in the trade) are rightly considered the smart money, those traders believe they know more about their market than anyone else and hence are to be copied.

But many of the commercials take positions because they have to – they are hedging their commercial activities. They are therefore **price-insensitive.** On the other hand, the small specs are the most price-sensitive with the hedge funds in the middle of the price-sensitivity scale.

This data is only useful to me at extremes of long/short ratios and is not a trade timing indicator for swing trades. It merely adds to the evidence I gather from my main trade timing tools.

www.cftc.gov

US economic reports

The US government issues a huge number of basic economic data, such as the US Unemployment Rate, Housing Starts, GDP figures, non-farm payrolls and so on. It is useful to keep a calendar handy to warn of upcoming important reports which could affect markets in the near-term. I use Bloomberg for this.

www.bloomberg.com

VIX

The VIX is the Chicago Board Options Exchange Volatility Index and is referred to as the Fear Index. A high reading indicates increased expectation of higher market volatility and vice versa.

www.cboe.com/vix

On the lighter side

Trading isn't all serious work – I hope. For a hilarious read here is an account of a young lady who stumbled into spread betting and somehow survived.

Bets and the City, by Sally Nicoll (Harriman House).

ADD TO YOUR HARRIMAN HOUSE TRADING LIBRARY

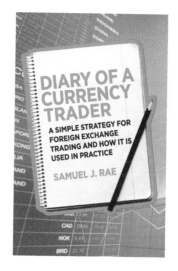

Lightning Source UK Ltd.
Milton Keynes UK
UKOW07f1533310116

267358UK00008B/32/P